The Outskirts of His Glory

Surprising places in God's creation that reveal who he is

Anna
JENSEN

Onwards and Upwards Publishers

3 Radfords Turf, Cranbrook, Exeter,
EX5 7DX, United Kingdom.

www.onwardsandupwards.org

First edition, published in the United Kingdom by Onwards and Upwards Publishers Ltd. (2019).

ISBN: 978-1-78815-690-5
Typeface: Sabon LT / Caslon Bd BT
Graphic design: LM Graphic Design
Photographs: pp. 7, 50, 102, 108 © Stephanie Bolstad

Printed in the United Kingdom.

Endorsements

Anna Jensen matches the beauty of the Southern African landscape with the beauty of her writing. Description and poetry work together to paint her joy and wonderment in God's creation. A book to gladden the soul.

Caroline Seed
CMS Mission Partner, Africa

In our 24/7 always-connected world it seems rare for someone to slow down enough to see things around them that speak of God's wonder. Anna is such an exception. This book helps us to see what is often right in front of us but we've missed in our hurry. Dallas Willard apparently once said that in order to grow in one's spirituality "[y]ou must ruthlessly eliminate hurry from your life, for hurry is the great enemy of spiritual life in our world today". Reading this will help you slow down and see the glory of God which in turn will cause you to worship, and no one ever stays the same when they worship. Use this book to wonder, worship and wait on God and you will find change takes place within you. Well done, Anna; this is a gift to those who read it.

Steve Campbell
Senior Pastor, Cambridge Community Church

Anna Jenson has produced a very original and delightful collection of some two dozen helpful and varied meditations. The format is very appealing; each meditation has a striking and relevant photograph, an interesting and informative travelogue of some part of Africa from which she draws out her varied spiritual lessons, an original and intriguing piece of poetry and a helpful prayer. It is all beautifully written, but the real joy in is the way she makes you feel the depth of her own eager perception of God in nature. It is infectious and makes you want to follow her lead. An excellent present.

Bob Dunnett
Retired Vice-Principal, Birmingham Bible College;
author of *Understanding the Times*

About the Author

Anna is a British ex-pat who moved to South Africa over twenty years ago, after meeting and marrying her husband, Craig, when living in Cambridge. They now live, together with their daughter Caragh and son Leal, a few kilometres north of Durban in a small coastal village where they can watch dolphins and whales at play. In 2008, Craig and Anna became the Lead Couple in the local church where they had been on eldership for several years; this they led until handing on the baton to another couple in 2017. Anna has spent many happy hours in an off-road four-by-four with Craig and the children, exploring the beauty of her adopted country and a few of its neighbours. It was after one such trip, to Zimbabwe, that Anna felt the call to 'write what you see in a book'. And so, a whole new adventure began.

More information about Anna and her story can be found at *www.annajensen.co.uk*, where you'll find a link to her blog '20 years an expat' together with a 'behind the scenes' look at the writing of this book. You'll also be able to hear Anna reading an extract or two.

Contents

Introduction

WHEN DID YOU LAST LISTEN TO THE GRASS GROW?! OR PAY attention to the song being sung by that bird who always visits the back garden in the afternoon? Often we become so waylaid by our own busyness and preoccupations, we fail to even notice these things, much less stop and pay attention to them.

Why does that matter? 'The Teacher' of Ecclesiastes declares that God has placed eternity in each of our hearts; we have a God-given longing to see beyond our limited horizon, to search deeper than the here and now. We are only fully satisfied when we glimpse, albeit 'through a glass, darkly'[1], that which we will eventually see 'face to face'[2].

Ezekiel had the great privilege of just such a glimpse. He describes his vision of Jesus:

> *And above the expanse over their heads there was the likeness of a throne, in appearance like sapphire; and seated above the likeness of a throne was a likeness with a human appearance. And upward from what had the appearance of his waist I saw as it were gleaming metal, like the appearance of fire enclosed all around. And downward from what had the appearance of his waist I saw as it were the appearance of fire, and there was brightness around him. Like the appearance of the bow that is in the cloud on the day of rain, so was the appearance of the brightness all around. Such was the appearance of the likeness of the glory of the Lord.*
>
> *Ezekiel 1:26-28*

Think about this for just a moment. The shimmering, ethereal beauty of a rainbow as it appears in the clouds on a grey, dark day – the accompanying sense of childlike wonder and pleasure, a joy that needs others to share in it, an eager searching to see more clearly – surrounding a throne on which sat what appeared to be a fire-man, burning gold, yellow, orange, red. And this was just the *appearance* of the *likeness* of

---

[1] 1 Corinthians 13:12 (KJV).

[2] *Ibid.*

God's *glory* – how much more incredible, indescribable, must God himself be? Little wonder Ezekiel fell to the ground in awe.

Not many of us experience visions like that! But God in his kindness has provided us with the means to take a peek at his glory on an everyday basis – through his creation. Paul writes in Romans that God uses creation to make himself visible and accessible to all;[3] Isaiah says the trees of the field shall clap their hands in joy; Jesus says the very stones on the ground are capable of worshipping him.

And Job declares:

> *He stretches out the north over the void and hangs the earth on nothing. He binds up the waters in his thick clouds, and the cloud is not split open under them. He covers the face of the full moon and spreads over it his cloud. He has inscribed a circle on the face of the waters at the boundary between light and darkness. The pillars of heaven tremble and are astounded at his rebuke. By his power he stilled the sea; by his understanding he shattered Rahab. By his wind the heavens were made fair; his hand pierced the fleeing serpent. Behold, these are but the outskirts of his ways, and how small a whisper do we hear of him! But the thunder of his power who can understand?*
>
> *Job 26:7-14*

The whispers of his ways are all around, all the time, beckoning us to fix our attention, to attune our ears, to quieten our hearts, so we may be captivated by him. We are called to be still and know that he is God, to abide in him, to seek him. My hope is this book will help us do just that.

In 'Thunderous Whispers', take a lighter-hearted exploration into some of those quirks of nature that indicate just how creative and fun-loving our God is; then take a slow meander through 'Pilgrim Wanderings', taking keener notice of what lies to the right and left of our paths. After this, spend some time pondering his 'Higher Ways' – his patience, his agelessness, his eternal purposes. For those times when the journey takes us along less refreshing routes, 'Determined Wrestlings' offers hope in the knowledge that the Lord has both a reason and a rescue in mind. And finally, be drawn into the magnificence that are his

---

[3] See Romans 1:20.

'Wonders Revealed', where just a foretaste of his brilliance is sufficient to undo us.

Come with me as I reflect on the *outskirts of his glory*.

Thunderous Whispers

There are so many ways that God whispers to us through his creation. Here in Southern Africa, those whispers are often as loud as shouts; quirks and oddities that draw immediate attention. A short drive around a well-populated game park will soon confirm the creative delight taken over the strangest of creatures – the wildebeest (or gnu), according to Zulu myth, comprised of the leftover parts of other animals; the giraffe, with the most ridiculous long neck and the ability to prise leaves from a clutch of thorns with a mere twist of the tongue; the painted beauty of an impala; or the trumpeted swagger of the elephant. As I've had the privilege of travelling many hundreds of kilometres around just a small corner of this glorious continent, I've been stirred to listen more attentively.

Baobab Valley

He has made everything beautiful in its time.

Ecclesiastes 3:11

THERE ARE TIMES WHEN WE ENCOUNTER SOMETHING SO contrary to our expectations, so opposite to our normal experiences, that we are pulled up short and forced to take a second look, a closer scrutiny.

There are a few ways to travel between South Africa and Zimbabwe, but by far the most popular takes the route through Limpopo Province to the border crossing at Beitbridge. Most people like to get to the border as early as possible on the morning of crossing, given that it can be a lengthy process, even on the best of days. However, there is a slight problem with this plan; there is no large urban area offering overnight accommodation to the weary traveller. Perhaps the closest, and most pleasant after a long day driving over a thousand kilometres from Durban, is a resort in Tshipise. This is a mere hundred or so kilometres to the border, so a great place to refresh and revive after a day in the car.

And why is it so great? Perhaps the hot springs found in the region have something to do with it! We chose to take a short stopover at Tshipise ourselves when taking our own road trip to Zimbabwe. Thankfully we'd had an earlier overnight stop in Johannesburg, and so were able to arrive less worn and weary at the resort early in the afternoon, enabling us a chance to enjoy what was on offer; which was, alongside the tennis courts and crazy golf course, a swimming pool heated exclusively by the influx of warm water from the thermal spring located on the property.

Our first priority, after unpacking our food and overnight bags, was to locate the spring itself. We set off, following pathways and signposts through the resort, until eventually we found a small bridge over what appeared to be a hole in the ground. And quite a smelly hole it was too! As we looked down, small clouds of steam rose from the water that bubbled up from below the rocks, bringing with them the stench of sulphur familiar in such locations. I've seen many little streams and rivers emerging from cracks and crevices, but it's certainly the first time I've seen one that is clearly not as ice cold as I would have usually expected; clouds of steam hovered above its surface.

After finding the spring itself, surrounded as it was with danger signs alerting would-be swimmers not to plunge into its burning depths, we wandered further along to find the swimming pool where a quick dip was definitely encouraged.

It was an eerie scene that greeted us as we rounded a corner and found the pool. What looked like a normal resort pool was in front of us, surrounded by lush grass lawns and paving stones. The changing rooms to one end were red brick, and equally normal. However, the vapour lazily rising above the surface of the water wasn't normal, and neither was the strange quiet that pervaded the air – the sounds of screaming and splashing that would be expected to accompany this sort of public space were strangely absent. Furthermore, there were warning signs everywhere, imploring bathers not to exert too much exuberance when swimming.

We entered the still, slightly sulphurous-smelling water with trepidation. It was the middle of winter, cold enough for our breath to fog when we spoke to each other. To be wading into a swimming pool, in the far north of the country under such conditions seemed completely ridiculous. Nevertheless, we continued and stepped into water so warm it could rival any evening's relaxing bath. We soon understood the request to not swim over-energetically – heat exhaustion would be a quick result. We made our slow progress along the length of the pool until, somewhere near the middle, there was a rush of water so hot we were forced to retreat a couple of paces. We had found the spring's pipe inlet.

That was the first unexpected surprise of our journey to the border. Our next came the following morning. Rising before dawn and making sure we were on the road as early as possible, we drove the half hour or so to Musina and the nearby border. On our way, as the sun rose, we noticed the strangest trees on either side of the road as we passed. Baobabs.

Baobabs are the most amazing, intriguing trees I have ever seen. Some have trunks so broad, the outstretched arms of a family of four can't quite reach round them. One is sizeable enough to host a small pub and its visitors. Then there are tiny, shrivelled-up ones, barely visible amongst the stature of their betters. We travelled along a 120 kilometre stretch of road, spanning the border between the two countries, and gave up counting how many we could see after about 150.

But it's not their great size variance, nor their proliferation in that one particular valley that fascinates; it's their shape. They look as though a child had given their carefully drawn picture of a tree to God and asked him to use it as a blueprint, but in their haste and excitement had presented the picture upside down. The grey trunks grow like branchless stumps until they reach a hair-like protrusion at the top, seeming like roots transplanted from their usual growing medium of soil and forced instead to suck nutrients from the air. Are their branches, then, buried deep underground, unable to wave free in the breeze? Even their location amidst scrubby, rocky ground seems wrong – how can anything grow to their enormous size in such seemingly inhospitable terrain? In fact, they are designed perfectly for the climate in which they prosper; their fibrous bark stores whatever water it draws up during the rainy season and utilises it later, either during the dry winter or during a more prolonged drought.

I love that God has created these wonderful examples of the weird and the strange, like hot springs and baobab trees. Their unexpectedness, their seeming so out of place, can stop us in our tracks and trip us up as we journey busily through life. They give us a chance to pause and reflect, to reassess what it is important and what, actually, is of little value. We are forced to acknowledge that God doesn't always do what we want in the way that we want, but that he is more than able to make a way regardless.

They also remind me that we are aliens and strangers in this world where we live, as the writer to the Hebrews testifies;[4] we aren't meant to fit in, to be the same as our surroundings. Rather, we should stand out, sometimes as strange or odd at first glance, but always bearing testimony to the way that God has turned our lives upside down by the saving intervention of the Cross and his son Jesus. Or is that right side up, just like a baobab?

---

[4] See Hebrews 11:13.

Topsy-Turvy

Today I feel all upside down
with feet that dance in brilliant ether
and a head that's buried deep.
To tell the truth, I'm topsy-turvy,
not right way round at all.

I've wriggling worms adorning my hair
and birds are tickling my toes.
My nose is feeling all bunged up
while my limbs are deliciously free.

'And what about me?' calls the spring in the rock.
I'm usually feeling so cool,
yet deep within, my belly is rumbling
and the liquid inside is near boiling.

And I have to admit the smell of my breath
is sadly somewhat unpleasant,
but the warmth that I bring to a winter's day chill
is welcomed by all those who enter.

It seems both of us are odd in some ways,
phenomena strange and unusual;
and yet, being placed here will maybe remind
that our Maker has love of surprise.
His pleasure in fun
and delight of the whimsy
will surely restore faith in his choosing
of you, for the Here and the Now.

For though you may feel
that you don't belong,
his ways are no mistake or gaffe.
and as perfectly pleasing as his purpose for us,
so too are the plans made for you.

PRAYER

Jesus, thank you that you know me and you love me.

Thank you that I am fearfully and wonderfully made by you, and you don't make mistakes.

Thank you for showing me the quirky and the strange in your creation so I may know that you delight in variety and difference.

Help me to trust you when I find myself feeling unusual and out of place, knowing that you have a reason for my being where I am today.

Thank you that you make all things beautiful in their time, and that includes me.

Joy

I came that they may have life and have it abundantly.

John 10:10

I SOMETIMES SUSPECT THAT THE LORD HAS A GREATER SENSE of humour than we think, and that heaven is a place of laughter as much as it is of worship and adoration. Not the little titters of polite appreciation but rambunctious roars and gleeful guffaws, burbling belly laughs of pure, untarnished joy. Revelation says there will be no more sorrowing or sighing, no more tears or sadness – what else will be in their place but smiles and delight?

But what about before we reach this delightful paradise? Jesus tells us not to worry about our lives, what we will eat or drink, or what we should wear. He states that birds never go hungry and the flowers are as beautifully clad as any courtier found in King Solomon's palace.[5] Is the implication perhaps that we too easily become concerned about things that don't matter, intense and uptight, when in fact we can be carefree and glad-hearted?

My daughter, Caragh, loves to go scuba diving; it is her greatest passion. Recently she was diving during the whale season here in South Africa, when humpback and sperm whales come closer to the coast to mate and have their young. As she and my husband were under the water, they could hear the whales nearby, apparently sounding not unlike mooing cows. After one such dive, she was chatting to one of the dive masters, asking about the whales' habit of throwing their bodies out of the water and smacking their tail fin down with such force that the thump can be heard several kilometres away. In reply to her 'Why do they that?', Ben, the dive master said, 'I think, just because it's fun and they like it'.

When we visited Namibia, we took a drive to the salt flats at Walvis Bay. On either side of a narrow causeway jutting out into the bay, pools of varying depth baked in the sun. Around the edges the crystalline salt deposits glinted as the evaporating water receded. In each pool there stood, some on both legs but many on one, flocks of pink and white flamingos, their heads bending gracefully down as they fished for their preferred snacks. Although it looked a beautiful, tranquil scene of sparkling light and feathered candy, the smell had us keeping the windows closed and the air conditioning on!

We left the salt pools behind and continued along the sand spur as it edged the harbour. Our destination was Pelican Point, the name of which alone made it sound worth an explore. The children took it in turns to sit on Craig's lap and drive the four-by-four over ridges of hardened sand,

[5] See Matthew 6:25-32.

much to their delight. Up ahead we gradually discerned various dark humps and lumps, stark against the paler beach. As we drew closer, we realised these were Cape fur seals – and thousands of them. There were big, fat lazy ones, cute little baby ones, some sleeping, some frantically lurching away from our approach. Some splashed round the edge of the water, taking a cooling dip in the chill of the ocean. A jackal lay off to one side of them, presumably waiting for a hapless infant to be separated from its family and so become lunch. But the greatest sight of all was the surfing seals! They raced down the edge of the curling waves, torpedoes visible in the clear aquamarine of the sea; they rushed and swooped and fell and swam back out again. Yes, there may have been purpose in the activity, such as catching food or strengthening lithe bodies for future journeys, but at its core there seemed to be the sheer joy and playfulness of tumbling through living liquid. We could almost see them grin.

Birds of prey seem to similarly surf effortlessly through their own 'waves' as they rise and fall on thermals of air. Our house overlooks the sea and I have often sat and watched the yellow-billed kites as they float high above, occasionally twitching their tails to better catch the up-draught or change direction. One day, I was watching as a couple of them glided by and was struck by how easy it looked. I felt the whispered nudge of the Holy Spirit as he gently challenged me about my own life – was I allowing myself to trust to the thermals of God as he leads me each day, to rise and dip in tune to his rhythms and patterns, rather than my own? Or was I working really hard to make it all happen, striving to accomplish a plan that only I had in mind? Had I, in fact, completely forgotten to simply enjoy the ride instead of constantly fretting about the destination?

Jesus says he has come to give life, and life in all its fullness;[6] a sense of enjoyment, of delight in the playful, is his gift to us. As we learn to laugh again, to embrace the pleasure of the simple, to escape, if only for a moment, from the intensity of the battle that undeniably rages, we in turn can become a gift to those around who don't yet know of his love, forgiveness and freedom.

---

[6] See John 10:10.

Full

When last did I tarry
in this way of waiting
letting waves speak wonders
and sun leave smiles?
To sit with no purpose
no plan
no plaything,
merely to capture a world as it passes.

A twist of a tail
and the wings of a kite –
tethered not by string or line –
catch the thermal draft of upward air;
then low, now high
in the sky.
Effortless entertainment;
delicious descent;
joy in the call to accompany.

Have I, with my burdens
my weighty concerns
become earth-tied and shackled
my heart not to soar with the ease of his breath;
forgotten to roller and coaster
and whoop with the shout
of the cared-for beloved?

In summer's haze of longer days
the lark I spy on high.
His aria the notes of purest praise;
a melody –
a hallejuah –
for heaven to receive.
While yellowed corn and browning soil
accept the drops of dew-like song
as earth absorbs the rain;
and rainbow-sound dances round.

Piercing and true.

Have I, my heart, forgotten
how to lift myself to sing
those love songs which have nested long?
Release them once again
that they may hover
loud and free.

Consider next the ocean's depths
bluer than that sky.
Hear, with me, a different tail –
another song –
the slap, the crash, the boom,
the wardrobe of a whale
as she nurses young
and makes a play to say,
'The big, the small, they all can thrive;
the Lord God made us all
to live, to love, to laugh;
to make a giant splash.'

Have I, instead, apologised
or thought I'm in the way?
Have shrunk myself that I might not disturb
the surface of the deep
when you have said to me to live,
be large,
be *me*?

Or how about those who surf
not on boards of man,
but using tails and flippers
and fins and feet;
they surge and twist and roll,
gathering speed
as,
frozen in the moment,

they seem a specimen locked in glass
happiness perfectly preserved;
then, foam-filled crash
and lost from view...
but not from heart or thought.

Could it be that all of this
is shown so I might see
this life with all its fulness
is your gracious
death-bought
gift –
for me?
And that I should live it
Full
and
Free.
Full
of laughter.
Free
to play and pray and worship;
to feel the ups and downs
the highs, the lows
the mountaintops and valleys.

Knowing that in you
just you
I am (w)holy complete.
Full.

PRAYER

Jesus, thank you that have come to give life and to give it abundantly.

Thank you that your joy is my strength.

Help me to love this life you have given me, to find delight and laughter in the things I see around me.

Help me to cast my cares onto you, knowing that you love me and will look after me, just as you do the birds of the air and the flowers of the field.

Help me to be a joy-giver to those I meet, just as you are to me.

The Buffelant

...having acknowledged that they were strangers and exiles on the earth.

Hebrews 11:3

WHILE VISITING FAMILY IN HARARE, WE WERE INVITED TO A small game park owned by friends of theirs. We accepted the invitation and set off in search of adventure.

We took a couple of hours to travel the few kilometres north of the city, travelling past field after field of now abandoned farm land. Sadly, the land redistribution policy of the early 2000s had led not to a newly-empowered black agricultural class, but rather to farm after farm of lost productivity. Neat, well-tended orchards and fields are now unpruned wild wastes, the hard work of decades and generations all but lost.

We arrived at the game park, a combined working farm and conservation scheme. Driving through the gates towards the accommodation, long, dusty brown grass swishing past the vehicles, we spied our first wildlife – a secretary bird marching its way purposefully across the veld, stamping its feet hard on the ground as it sought its prey of small rodents and reptiles. It was our first ever sighting of this elusive bird and its presence elicited no small degree of excitement amongst us.

We off-loaded our four-by-fours, dumping our stuff in our little thatched cabins, and went in search of dinner. It was a lovely evening, freezing cold as only the bush at night in winter can be. There were fires lit both outside and in, and a dining table laden with roast meat, potatoes and fresh vegetables.

The next morning, after what had seemed a rather long night of trying to keep warm, we grabbed an early breakfast and headed out to the awaiting open-air game viewing vehicle, wrapping ourselves in blankets against the morning chill.

We drove into the reserve proper, stopping to observe any sort of wildlife. The secretary bird from the day before had disappeared, leaving us feeling even more delighted at our previous success in seeing it.

After a while we stopped on the road in a large open area, surrounded by a herd of buffalo. Pretty normal usually, but distinctly unusual on this occasion. For there, happily grazing amongst these horned beasts, was an elephant. No ordinary elephant, we were to discover. Orphaned as a youngster, the family, having no other elephants at the time, had placed her in the temporary care of a herd of buffalo. Only, the temporary had become permanent, and 'the buffelant', as she was affectionately known, had become an integral part of the herd.

Several attempts had been made to reintroduce her to elephant life, placing her with a couple of elephants the farm later acquired. She remained aloof from them, isolated in her belief that, despite very obvious appearances, she wasn't in fact one of them. She felt herself to be buffalo, and was soon pining for the familiar, whereupon she was returned to the herd.

Although identifying so strongly with the buffalo, in her mannerisms and instincts she was very much elephant. Elephant society is matriarchal, with the dominant female responsible for, amongst other things, the discipline of the herd. Somewhere deep in her psyche, despite never have grown up in a normal elephant community, the buffelant knew this. Even though buffaloes are quite the reverse, and it is the dominant bull who wields the most power, the buffelant carried out her duties as matriarch admirably, restraining the younger bulls when they became too aggressive, especially around any young calves. She had even been known to trample a couple of renegades to death as the ultimate punishment.

I mentioned this to a friend the other day, and her response was, 'How can we not see that God has placed his mark and design on all creatures, regardless of the environment in which they are found?' Once more, I am reminded that he has put eternity in the hearts of all men, that our identities are intimately connected to our creator. We are made in the image of God, not like any other creature on the face of the earth. We were made for heaven, we were made for heavenly relationship between ourselves and God, and between each other, and something deep within the inner beings of all of us knows this. We, like the buffelant, are living in a herd where we don't belong; our citizenship, as Paul says in Philippians 3:20-21, is elsewhere. And just as the buffelant never fully fits into her adopted herd, neither will we fully fit in on an earth not yet completely set free from the power of sin.

So why are we here? Why can't God take us to heaven the moment we accept Jesus as our Lord and Saviour, restoring to us the depth of relationship we were designed for? The buffelant sticks out like the proverbial sore thumb amongst her buffalo family, no matter how much she may think she blends in. We should also, having encountered Jesus, be unable to blend in with our friends and families who don't yet know him; the difference he has made to our lives should be as instantly obvious.

Whilst the buffalo will never become elephants thanks to the reforming presence of the buffelant, this isn't the same for the herd around us; our intentional presence within whatever communities we find ourselves in will bring about change and restoration.

Who Am I?

I think there's something not right,
something that doesn't quite fit.
Perhaps I'm just tall
or are you all short?
Whatever, our eyes seldom meet.

And why, I must ask, do you bend when you eat
or chew with your nose on the ground?
When surely, my friend, to lift to your mouth
your handy proboscis, with all it can hold
is far better manners,
and easier too?

Another 'for instance' are those horns on your head
which really do look like a fancy new hair-do
piled up on top and curled at the side.
Mine, it would seem, are not quite the same
growing, instead, from my gum.

And those ears that you sport are ridiculously little;
they can't even waft and create
the breeze that you need
in the heat of the African sun.

I wonder sometimes if I really belong
or whether elsewhere is my home?
And yet, it is here with you I abide.
Who knows, it just may be
that my being here has a reason;
as learning from me
your own ways may change
until you are known
as an elephalo.

Prayer

Jesus, thank you that my citizenship is with you in Heaven and that I'm not meant to feel fully at home here on earth.

Today I choose to be recognised as belonging to you.

Help me to be your representative to those around me, knowing you have set times and exact places for me to be where I am.

Draw others into your family through me.

Quirky Community

A new commandment I give to you, that you love one another: just as I have loved you, you also are to love one another. By this all people will know that you are my disciples, if you have love for one another.

John 13:34-35

COMMUNAL LIVING – WHAT IMAGES DOES THAT PHRASE conjure up? For me, I must confess, I think of a shabby lounge with India-cotton-covered couches inhabited by long-haired, long-skirted vegans! Isn't my stereotyping terrible?

When we visited Israel a few years ago, I saw something of communal living that gave me a whole new perspective. We visited a work associate of my husband Craig who lived in a kibbutz, that great farming and settlement model developed and adopted by newly-returning Jews to their ancestral homeland. It was a real eye-opener.

Our host headed up a fructose manufacturing plant that is owned and run by the kibbutz. Normally this sort of position would be associated with a considerable degree of prestige and its associated perks. In the kibbutz, however, the most senior manager was paid pretty much the same as the newest apprentice or cleaner. This equality continued into their allocation of homes within the village – no one house was larger or more luxurious than the other, and no home was owned by its occupants.

We were taken on a brief tour by our host and his wife. First, we visited the communal dining room. They explained that, until fairly recently, all meals had been cooked and served here rather than by individuals in their homes. The whole community had come together every day for breakfast, lunch and supper. Upcoming social activities were advertised on the noticeboards; nothing and no one was left out.

At the far end of the dining hall was a small meeting room and library, which we were shown with some pride. Here there were photos and documents depicting the founding of the kibbutz, snaps of pioneers intent on transforming the obviously rocky and barren landscape into fertile arable fields. The reason for the pride soon became apparent – our host's wife's parents were amongst the original settlers and community leaders.

Emerging through the external double doors back into the sunlight, some newly built houses just outside the kibbutz fence were pointed out to us. These, it was explained, belonged to some of the children of the current kibbutz residents, young people who had different ideas about property ownership and future security; they wished to continue living in the area but wanted to enjoy the benefits of a property which belonged, ultimately, to them and not to the whole community.

After walking for a little longer, we retraced our steps to where we were to have lunch in the family home (indicative of how the times have changed even for the most committed communal participant). As we chatted over lunch, I mentioned that I liked their home. The wife said sadly that it was rather small, having only the one bedroom. I was surprised to hear that, as I knew they had children who were now grown up and independent but who had presumably needed bedrooms there at some point. The couple went on to explain that at the time when they were raising their young family, children didn't actually live with their families. Rather, they stayed in a specially designated children's house elsewhere in the village, visiting home only between school and supper each day. Mothers would take turns to care for all the children in the house on a rota basis – even parenting was thus a communal responsibility.

To my Western, individualistic thinking, this was shocking. But there was sense in it; the commune was situated in hostile territory, right on the newly-designated border. Skirmishes and gun battles were common, so keeping the children in one safe location was wise. Furthermore, working and transforming the land was long, hard work. Adults could be dedicated to their tasks for several hours without the regular interruption of family duties. Certainly there were drawbacks, and our hostess seemed to feel she had missed out on connection with her own parents as a result of this policy, but it did result in the desired establishment of a thriving permanent settlement.

Obviously, this is an extreme example of community, developed by people with political motives as much as religious fervour. What of the wider creation, the realm of God's design and planning? We discovered community living on a grand scale a few years ago when travelling across South Africa towards Namibia.

We had set off from Bloemfontein on a cold, crisp winter's morning to drive along previously unencountered roads towards the border post. Long straight kilometres of tar stretched ahead of us, flat dusty farmland as far as we could see on either side. In the distance, a blueish tinge indicated the mountains for which we were headed. Running parallel to the road were the posts and wires that delivered electricity to the surrounding farms and villages.

As we gazed out of the window, we started to notice odd piles of grass and straw leaning against the electricity poles. In some places, the post of a fence or trunk of a tree was engulfed by these shaggy piles. Some were a dull brown colour, looking like so many abandoned thatch cottages; others seemed more recently constructed, brighter and paler yellow. We were utterly perplexed – what on earth were they? We wondered if they were somehow part of a famer's feeding strategy for his livestock, but as there were no cattle or sheep that we could see, this seemed unlikely. As we became more and more intrigued, we started to look a little more closely at them, even stopping by the side of the road to investigate and take some photos. To our surprise, as we watched a number of small birds flying in and out of them, we realised they were birds' nests.

But these were the biggest birds' nests we had ever seen. Some of them were two metres high and heavy enough to break the branches of trees or bend previously upright posts and poles. It turns out that these are nests made by the appropriately named 'sociable weaver', the largest of all birds. Within their chambers, which can number as many as five hundred, there live generations of weaver birds, each pair with their offspring occupying different 'rooms' – the outer during the day, when there is need for cool; and the inner at night, when warmth is required. Not only do these weavers live in the same nest as each other, they also assist one another when raising their young. Communal parenting once more.

However, it is not only the little weavers who inhabit these magnificent haystacks. Other small birds, such as finches, move in temporarily during the breeding season, whilst chats regularly spend the night. Owls, falcons and other large birds perch atop the 'roof' when in search of prey, and snakes and other reptiles enjoy the delights of a well-stocked restaurant at meal times.

Jesus told his disciples that it would be by their love for one another that the world would know who his followers are. In the book of Acts, the believers held everything in common, both for the well-being of the people and the furtherance of the gospel.[7] Whilst I'm not sure I would be able to live on a kibbutz, I do recognise the need to perhaps change the way I connect with other Christians, with my brothers and sisters. Those sociable weavers indicate that God clearly loves community and family. He is, after all, that greatest of mysteries, Three in One; Father, Son and Holy Spirit. Those giant nests serve as a fresh reminder that, though it may seem hard, or even impossible, for us to live in the kind of community God would wish, with him we should remember all things are possible.

---

[7] See Acts 4:32.

Welcome to the Nest

Welcome, come in, take a seat,
can I make some tea?
Yes, it is a little cramped and crowded
and Piccadillian in its circus bustle
but we've come to not mind
or to fuss.

What did you say?
The noise, I'm afraid,
quite baffling to start with, I know.
But it's cheerful, we find,
rambunctious and raucous
but real.

Who's that, did you ask;
the one sitting right over there?
Why, that is my aunt, Mary Chat –
or is it in fact Uncle Finch?
We've such a large family
reposed in this home
that sometimes it's too hard to tell.
Ah, that thud on the roof,
a little unnerving,
but really no need for alarm;
our neighbour, Sir Falcon
returning to perch
while surveying for something to eat.

Yes, somehow this all works –
of each other we're terribly fond –
an example we make
of community care
with never a one being lost or too lonely.

And when predators come
as of course they will do,
together we stand to repel;

each one belonging
  in our various ways;
all needed, all cherished
  all counted.

Prayer

Jesus, thank you that you have placed me in a family, in a community with others who know you.

Thank you that our love for one another comes first from your great love for us.

Help me to be committed to the well-being of others, to pray for them and cheer them on.

Help me to call on them when I need help, realising that I don't have to do everything by myself.

In this way, may we be attractive to those who don't yet know you, drawing them closer to you by our active love for you and each other.

Pilgrim Wanderings

We are called to be pilgrims, travellers through this temporal life towards an eternal destination of peace, joy and wonder. At times, our passage is easy and enjoyable, a gentle stroll through undulating parklands, sheltered from the fiercest of elements and accompanied by the pleasantest of friends. At other times, it's a hard slog through the toughest terrain, battling away on our own and struggling not to give up with every step. Once more, the perfect creator who is our loving Father has left us clues for the journey, a treasure map etched into the very landscape around us, guiding and spurring us onwards. Those whose hearts are set on the destination, though we walk through valleys of tears, or wrestle our way up the highest of mountains, will find pools of refreshment and encouragement along the path, if only we will look.

Because You're 'Gorge-eous'

So God created man in his own image, in the image of God he created him; male and female he created them.

Genesis 1:27

I REALLY ENJOY WALKING ALONGSIDE RIVERS, WHETHER they be still, calm waters of secluded green or the rushing and roaring of fast-flowing waterfalls and rapids. One of my favourite riverine locations though must be a gorge, with its steep sides dropping precipitously from great heights to the ribbon of blue and silver that is the water cutting its way steadily towards the sea. There is something mysteriously mesmerising about a slash in the landscape created by the softness of water exploiting a weakness in the strength of rock.

The most impressive water-filled gorge I've visited, in size at least, must be that which runs away from the bottom of Victoria Falls. The foaming, deafening pool of descending Zambezi River gradually settles down and organises itself into formation, meandering more sedately towards its final, oceanic destination. As it does so, it bends and winds through the passageways of cliffs that form its walls, leaving beaches of shingly deposits on some sides, scouring away the rock on the shorter, sharper inside turns. It soon disappears from sight, lost to its own world of adventures, watering countless fields, quenching countless thirsts.

More recently, we visited a less impressive-seeming gorge just a few hours south of Durban at Port Edward. We had decided to take a weekend break away in our caravan, taking a couple of surf skis for added entertainment as we were to be staying right on the edge of the Mtamvuna River. It is a campsite we've visited on several occasions, perhaps the most memorable being a New Year's Day of several years ago following a week of heavy rain. The campsite had been full of New Year's Eve celebrants and the ground had turned to ankle-deep mud. It was truly revolting! I think I have an idea of what trench-foot must have been like.

Anyway, on this occasion the weather was fine and the campsite green and pleasant. In addition to the water sports planned for the few days, we had also decided to explore the river from the top, where an area of trails and protected meadowland ran along the edge of the gorge. We checked out the maps and suggested walks in the area, and set off, walking directly from the campsite.

The first part of the walk took us through some dense indigenous forest. Tree roots criss-crossed our path, tripping us at every opportunity. Branches from the same trees sought to catch our hats or hair. We clambered and climbed our way steadily upward, a local park ranger our guide as he walked home for his lunch break.

Eventually we emerged from the trees into a field swaying with long grass and bright with flowers. The path skirted the edge, then began to climb a little more. By now, the river was far below us, out of sight, though not quite out of earshot. The ranger bid us farewell as he reached his home, describing to us the way we should proceed to reach the path along the gorge itself. We followed his instructions and came finally to the plateau, a wide, flat area with trees off to the right and the steep drop down to the river on our left. The path was clearly visible as a sandy, stony depression making its way amongst the short plants and grasses.

Our first stop was a decked viewing area, which could also be reached by driving and parking at the top rather than heaving on foot up the incline. We were rather proud of our achievement, as a couple of other visitors emerged from the treeline and made their short, easy way towards us. Far below us ran the river, with sandy banks and rock-induced rapids laid out in silent tableau. On each side, the gorge rose in a riot of plants and bushes and trees, a dense carpet of colour and texture adorning the rock face. Above flew a couple of raptors, unidentifiable against the brightness of the sky.

Our research before the excursion had indicated that the area we were exploring was home to more species of flora and fauna than any other in South Africa. It was a treasure-trove of botanical jewels; so we were told. Sadly, none of us are very good with plant-life identification. We continued our walk, stopping for a photo here and there, breaking for lunch on a conveniently chair-shaped rock, totally oblivious to the value of all that we were passing. It was undeniably rich and beautiful – but priceless? We really couldn't say.

And I got to thinking. In all God's creating fervour at the start of time, it was only on the completion of Adam and Eve that he declared, 'It is *very* good'[8] – up until then, everything had been denoted 'good'. Humans, you and I, are made exclusively and wonderfully in the image of God himself; we are unique, we are priceless, we are 'very good'. And even when we have messed up, excluding ourselves from the very thing we were meant for – friendship with this creator God – he still said, 'It is very good,' and provided us with a way back into relationship, through Jesus. The life-blood of the Son of God himself was offered, and accepted, as the necessary payment for restoration. Jesus died on a cross, was buried in a tomb and was gloriously raised back to life all so that you

[8] See Genesis 1:31.

and I could be reconnected with the love of the God who made us 'very good'.

Yet how often do I walk along the path of life, surrounded as it is by the many and the varied, and yet look only in front of me, never to the left or right of where I'm going? Worse still, how often do I look but not notice? See but not understand? I didn't know how rare and valuable some of the flowers and plants were that we passed on our walk that day; I find it too easy to forget how rare and valuable the people are whom I pass every day: the lady at the supermarket checkout; the guy driving in the car next to mine, listening to jazz at top volume; the children in the playground, their parents at the gate. Each have their stories, their trials and their joys. Over each, God shouts, 'It is very good.'

I could take the time to learn botany, to look at pictures of flowers and plants and learn to identify what the name is for each; I could revisit the area, take photos, go on guided walks with specialists. In truth, I'm very unlikely to do that. I just don't have the passion. But will I learn the lesson I was taught there? To have passion for, and compassion on, the people I pass; to take the time to learn their names, to identify each one, no matter how different or how strange, as priceless and precious. To walk slowly and carefully, knowing the journey to be richer, more brightly coloured, more textured, as I too say, 'It is very good.'

As I pass

I have walked
wandered
stumbled
past you
so many times;
blind, I think, to even your presence;
unaware, certainly, of your beauty.

I have fixed my attention on a point before me,
the destination, the end,
not the process;
the place the path is going
hurriedly more important
than the steps I tread today.

I have blended you with your neighbour,
labelled you both the same;
failed to see where the one has end
or where the other starts.

I've gazed across a landscape,
blurred the intricacy of individuality;
seen just one colour, one hue
instead of seeing you.

And even as I've hummed along
whistling while I walk
I've drowned the lilt and melody
of all the songs you've sung.
Deafened by my thoughts of me,
I've missed the call of you.

You, whose voice my Lover loves
more unique than every snowflake,
bought with all of heaven's treasure
more priceless than a pearl;
the masterpiece in the artist's collection
which demands I stop
notice
remark
cry, 'Look, come over here
to see what I have seen'.

To raise a flag of recognition
a banner unfurled
a royal standard lifted;
that other travellers and tourists
pilgrims and passers-by
may not
like me
fail to recognise the significance of you.

Prayer

Father, thank you that you have created every individual in your own likeness, that each person I meet is precious to you.

Help me to see others as you do, highly valued and treasured.

Forgive me for the times I've been unloving and dismissive, either deliberately or through a lack of understanding.

Thank you that there is beauty in each one, if I will only take the time to look.

Mountains Made Miniature

The mountains melt like wax before the Lord, before the Lord of all the earth.

Psalm 97:5

WHILST I ENJOY WALKING ALONGSIDE RIVERS, I AM NOT A great fan of mountain climbing! Unfortunately for me, Durban is a mere couple of hours from some of the most magnificent peaks and summits of the Great Escarpment which runs the length of South Africa. Here, the Drakensberg Mountains form a dragon's spine of pointy erosion-resistant basalt which runs along the Lesotho/KwaZulu-Natal border. For most Durbanites, at least those that I know, these peaks are a retreat from the manic busyness of the city, they are the one place where snow may fall during winter, and the mountains are meant to be climbed and conquered.

When visiting the Berg, as the area is affectionately known, the intrepid mountaineer starts on the lower slopes, staying in accommodation ranging from luxury hotel to unelectrified campsite. Our personal favourite for many years was a small, secluded camping area at the base of Cathedral Peak, reached after a long, twisting drive through the community of rural homesteads that hugged the river valley. Care had to be taken to avoid goats, cows or young children as they all unpredictably wandered who knew where. Slow and heavy trucks or pick-ups had to be cautiously negotiated around as they ground to a near-halt up the steep inclines. Eventually a cattle grid is crossed and humanity is left behind. The mountains are revealed in all their isolated splendour, the weight of life slips from the shoulders and deep breaths of relief are sighed. On a little further, and the campsite was in a small clump of trees near the river.

'Campsite' is perhaps a slightly grandiose term for the facilities offered! There were flattened patches of grass spaced at intervals under the trees, with a red brick ablution, or toilet and shower block, occupying pride of place in the centre. With no electricity available, the water was heated each day by a fire that was lit every morning by camp staff. The fire would smoke and blaze for hours, resulting in piping hot water emitting from the showers when needed towards the end of the day. Everywhere was cloaked by the somehow comforting smell of woodsmoke. Late in the afternoon, other fires would be lit by campers preparing for a relaxing evening of lazy cooking.

From this campsite there were a couple of main hiking options. One was to take a cheat drive in the car up the nearby forestry road and embark on the walk a good few kilometres further along than was strictly fair. This then allowed for a reasonably gentle walk along the contour path until a steeper final section led the way to a disused forestry hut, complete with outdoor toilet-with-a-view. The path did continue far up the mountain, but we always turned around at this point.

The other option was a mammoth hike from the car park a little further up the road from the campsite, right to the top of Cathedral Peak itself. Not for the faint-hearted or unfit, I have only conquered a short section of this journey, and that equipped only with a chocolate bar and orange for sustenance. I was not a happy hiker!

Along with the campsite, the other accommodation in this secluded area of national park is the Cathedral Peak Hotel. This is an exclusive and somewhat pricey hotel which we used to love visiting on special occasions. Every morning the buffet tables in the restaurant groaned under the weight of fresh fruits, yoghurts, pastries, cold meats and hot sides for the bacon and eggs served; evening saw a similar festival of overindulgence displayed and consumed. From the hotel, more short day walks are available, which give the taste of mountain adventure without quite as much effort required.

There are aspects to being in the mountains that I love – the sense of ageless permanence, the way the light shifts and changes throughout the course of a day, revealing new colours and shapes as the sun moves along its course. There can be a deep peace, on a still day with little breeze, when even the song of the insects sounds loud in the silence. Or there can be wild, terrifying symphonies of crashing thunder, whitest lightning, bucket-loads of rain. At night, the sky is alive with stars not visible in a city, their cold white gleams paled only by the colder shine of a full moon. The smallness of our lives and its worries, our cares and concerns are highlighted by the looming, brooding presence of mightiness. It is humbling and awe-inspiring.

But mountains can also be energy-draining in their vastness. An hour of plodding along and one feels no nearer the summit than one did at the start of the day. Depending on the terrain through which the path leads, there can be little relief from a hotly blazing sun or little respite from the toil of a steep climb. The legs hurt on the way up, the knees on the way down. Often the path is only wide enough to travel in single file, so a great deal of a day can be spent looking at the heels of the companion ahead, rather than happily chatting the time away together. Worse still, the climax of the effort often reveals, not a top-of-the-world, nowhere-else-to-climb exhilaration, but rather a vista of higher, harder peaks which tease laughingly at the exhausted mountaineer.

And although changeless and eternal-seeming, the character of a mountain may transform in an instant. Clouds begin to appear as fluffy white cotton balls right on the top; a gentle breeze starts to pick up. Within moments, the white fluff is replaced with darkly threatening grey, the wind has started to swirl the dust on the path, and rain – or worse, snow or hail – starts to fall. Shelter is urgent; good clothes, paramount. The unprepared can be left exposed and in danger in minutes. Similarly, a day can fade into night-time pitch darkness with surprising speed once the sun dips below the horizon. The temperature rapidly drops, despite the heat of a summer's day, and the need to get back to the car or pitch a tent becomes vital.

Most of us find ourselves confronted by metaphorical mountains at some time or another in our lives. They might be the mountains of ill-health, or financial troubles, or relationship issues. Or they could be the more corporately-experienced mountains of international economic or political change, wars, civil unrests, protests and insecurities. Regardless of their source, these peaks are just as real in their size and intimidatory abilities as the Drakensberg. They may seem to represent nothing except travail, hardship, effort, exhaustion. We become overwhelmed by their unmoving bulk, by our own complete insignificance in the face of such unconquerable loftiness.

However, just like the Drakensberg, or the Alps, or the Himalayas, they are part of the texture and beauty our creator has given as gifts to us. There are few better ways to get strong or fit than to firstly, prepare to climb, then secondly, actually climb, a steep mountain! The monotony of a flatland is sweetly broken by the insertion of a hill. Whilst I don't particularly like climbing them, I do love basking in the magnificence of a summit's enormity.

Perhaps it is all a matter of perspective. In May of this year, I flew to Cape Town for a weekend visit with a dear friend. The trip down was amazing – clear skies the whole way allowed a view from my window seat of some of the most mountainous regions of South Africa. In places, snow glinted as it reflected the sun's rays. There were shadows and highlights, rivers, gorges, peaks and summits, seeming almost two-dimensional from such a height. Each range seemed beautifully carved and crafted, a sculpture of colour and pattern created with skill, patience and love. There was nothing intimidating, nothing devastating about them. Rather, their exquisite design and the very fact of their stolid greatness caused me to worship the One who is infinitely more. Read

Psalm 97. There's no better way to say it. In the presence of him who is Lord of the whole earth, the mountains melt like wax. Let us lift our eyes beyond the heights and declare, 'My help comes from the Lord, the maker of heaven and earth. He will not allow my foot to slip, he will be my keeper and my shade at my right hand, he will guard my coming and my going, both now and for evermore.'[9]

Perspective

From up here they are carved by a craftsman;
they are the wrinkles of melted, set wax
like jam being tested for readiness;
they are bowls holding snow
and goblets of water.

But down there they are the bringers of insignificance,
the harbingers of a majesty beyond me;
they are that which dwarfs,
brings perspective.
Ageless, ancient
unmoving, unchanging,
undaunted, uncowed.
They are to be overcome.
To be conquered.
To be endured.
To be feared.

From here they are the steps and the stairs;
they are the eddies and flows
the tumbles and spirals
of water become rock, become stone.

They are the deep ocean floor
exposed to the air.
They are dragons' spines and dinosaurs' tales;
they are tabletops and runways.

---

[9] Psalm 121:2-8.

Cascades of light and dark
        of sunshine and shade.

They are living and breathing,
        hills still alive with the sound of music.

Carry me, lift me, draw me
        higher with you to see
            these mountains I face,
                have to climb,
                want to move,
            are but patterns in a landscape
            giving texture and context,
                challenge, reward;
    that though they are mighty to me,
        with you,
            who is more,
        they are playgrounds and playthings
            created for delight, not for dread.
So I, with this view and the faith that it brings
        may say to the mountain, 'Be moved to the sea.'
And it will.

Prayer

Father, thank you that you are Lord of all, that you are seated in heavenly places and that what seems so large and immovable to me is small and conquerable to you.

Help me to have eyes that see the grandeur of you in comparison to the insignificance of my difficulties, problems or challenges; that they would melt like wax in your presence.

Help me to continue to have this perspective when I interact with others who need encouragement when faced with their own mountains.

Project Grand

Then the Lord said to me, "You have seen well, for I am watching over my word to perform it."

Jeremiah 1:12

THERE'S A SONG BY THE AMERICAN CHRISTIAN BAND *THIRD Day* that starts, 'Standing on the edge of a canyon...' That's exactly what we did on first arriving in Namibia – stood on just a little of the edge of the Fish River Canyon.

However, before standing on its upper edge, we first descended to the canyon's floor. We drove down along steep declines between high walls of rockface, avoiding the boulders and scree which had come adrift over years and now lay beside the road. Eventually we reached the campsite at Ai-Ais and climbed out of the car.

It was chilly in the shade of the trees that were dotted around, but as we wandered towards the sunny patches nearby, we soon warmed up. The sky was brilliant azure, interspersed here and there with a few drifting white clouds. The gorge rose in majestic grey opposite the flatter camping area, divided by the gently flowing river; behind us, the sounds of a resort in holiday swing.

We didn't stay long, as we were anxious to complete the drive to what, we hoped, would be the more impressive top of the canyon. We retraced our journey out of the valley to seek the entrance to the National Park through which we would have to drive to reach our destination. Once found, we paid our entrance fees and continued onwards.

The landscape around us was flat and somewhat barren; just some winter grasses and shrubs could be seen. It seemed to take us an age to reach the viewing platform we'd been told to visit first. Finally, it appeared; a dark, very man-made shape on the horizon.

We found the car park and, for the second time that day, climbed out of the car and made our way up the steps to see the view. And discovered our efforts worthwhile. For as far we could see, stretching out to right, left and front was a topography that could only be marvelled at. The ground level remained the same as it had been for the last couple of hours, but now, rather than continuing into the distance, deep incisions disturbed its surface. Kilometres across, each gash twisted and turned leaving crescents and loops of absence; columns and pillars of the more resilient rock standing proud and tall, as if proving their superior strength.

We spent most of the rest of the day hopping in and out of the car, driving to another spot and checking the view from that perspective. The children were less than impressed with how long this all seemed to be taking, given that, to them at least, it was all the same regardless. But it was the huge scale of this massive feature that kept Craig and me hungry to see more. The ravine is the largest of its kind in Africa and is about 160 kilometres long and up to twenty-seven kilometres wide. In some places, the sheer drop is as much as 550 metres deep; from the top, the river we had just stood beside seemed a silent line on a page. It was too far to discern accurately if a still, dark shape was a rock, a shrub or a resting hiker.

After a while, we found a spot to sit for a picnic, giving ourselves time to absorb the immensity of our surrounds. The silence was tangible, with just the sound of the breeze in our ears. As we looked more closely, we noticed hardy little plants and flowers growing in the cracks of the rock. Stripes of colour alternated with one another as they decorated what had seemed a wall of solid grey. The afternoon sunlight adorned some areas with a golden glow, abandoned others to their colder, shadier fate.

It was an overwhelming sight. We were so small, so insignificant, perched on the edge of this formation of wonder. We couldn't see another person; there was no sign of human life or habitation. It was just us and this vista of splendour.

Two thoughts struck me as we sat and pondered. This canyon is ancient, and it took a really long time to get from flat, level plain to incised ravine. God oversaw the whole process, watched it develop from a stream to a river to a floodplain to a gorge; saw every waterfall, every spring, every landslide and rockfall. He watches over us with even greater care and concern, intimately aware of each crisis, each breakthrough. I believe he cheered over the formation of the Fish River Canyon, but I believe he cheers over us even louder.

And then, if rocks can be split apart, eroded, worn down by the persistent push and flow of water, how much more can the hardened heart or the tough situation be moulded and shaped, carved and sculpted by the persistent flow of God's love? That mere water, running steadily on its way to the sea, could produce such enormous fissures and cracks was mind-numbing; that God can take the heart of stone that resides within my chest and transform it to a heart of flesh is mind-blowing.

As Jeremiah heard, God is watching over his word to make sure it accomplishes that for which he has purposed.[10] Sometimes we think it's taking too long, it's just too slow a process for us to believe there's anything happening. Other times it seems too wild, too extravagant – God speaks that we will change the world, but this seems too

[10] See Jeremiah 1:2.

outrageously beyond our grasp to be seriously believed and held onto. The Fish River Canyon is a glorious reminder that God is not slow in keeping his promises; a thousand years to him is nothing. And grand scale projects are well within his abilities, whether they be shaping landscapes or lives.

Timelessness

Unveiled here before me
the miracle of change
as ageless as the time outside which you stand;
a plain and a ridge-top
inverted to valley and trough;
a stone-heavy heart caressed into flesh
and the grave becomes the place of my life.

The vitality of you
slashes through the monotony of me,
creating instead the delight of surprise
and the twist and the turn of a mystery.
You wend your way
through the chink in my armour
and soften what I thought was so solid,
penetrating deeper through this impregnable wall
opening a chasm
for a flood to come in,
flourishing and nourishing
me.

Prayer

Father, thank you that you are eternal and timeless, that what seems like a thousand years to me is but a day to you.

Thank you that you have a plan and a purpose for my life that you are fashioning in your own time.

Help me to trust that you know my dreams and have heard my prayers.

Help me to be patient while you work, both in my own life and in the lives of others I'm connected to.

Diamonds and Jewels

"Surely there is a mine for silver, and a place for gold that they refine ... But where shall wisdom be found? And where is the place of understanding?"

Job 28:1,12

I LIVED FOR SEVERAL YEARS, UNTIL I WAS ABOUT TWELVE, near the Peak District in Derbyshire. We would often take a Sunday afternoon drive to one of our favourite beauty spots and have a walk followed by a little picnic or visit to a teashop (hot buttered toasted teacakes were my particular favourite). If we had visitors or wanted to travel further afield to a more unusual location, we would travel the twenty-five kilometres or so to the Blue John Caves at Castleton. A complex of caves running deep into the landscape, they are considered by some to be amongst the finest caves accessible to the general public in the whole of Western Europe. Here, Britain's rarest mineral, the Blue John stone, was discovered by the Romans about two thousand years ago. It has been mined, primarily by hand, ever since. We never made it down the caves as children, but the reason we loved going there was to see the shops! Displayed in their brightly lit windows were all manner of twinkling, sparkling objects and trinkets. Blue stones encased in silver or gold winked like lazy eyes to passers-by. Miniature rainbows burst from their polished edges, enticing purchasers indoors to discover what other gleaming treasures might be found. Oh, how my sister and I longed to be purchasers!

Several years later, as a student and long after we'd moved away from the area, I revisited with a friend. We'd embarked on a walking / youth hostelling holiday together, exploring various places of interest as we journeyed. On one particular day, we set out for Castleton and the caves. We trudged across hills and down valleys, following the winding road from one village to the next. Eventually, we reached our destination.

After an obligatory sit down and cup of tea, we were all set for the next part of the adventure – a visit underground. We paid our entrance fee and joined the group heading into the caves. My main recollection is darkness, as we made our way along narrow passages and into hidden spaces far from the bustle and light of the street above. At one point, we arrived in a large, open chamber, where the guide exhorted us to gather around. He then switched the lights off; complete and total blackness the result.

Once the lights were restored, we continued on our way, past huge pointed stalactites dripping from the ceiling to join their columnar, stalagmite counterparts which grew upward from the floor. The whites and pale yellows of the limestone gleamed coldly wherever they were caught in the glare of carefully-positioned floodlights; vast subterranean palaces carved by centuries of rushing, gushing water now visited by mere mortals such as us.

More recently, as a family we toured the Cango Caves in South Africa, which run along the foothills of the Swartberg Mountains in the Little Karoo. The visitor is first led by an experienced guide through an uninspiring passageway and down a stairway with bannisters. Darkness, again, is the predominant sensation. Eventually, the guide stops the party and begins to tell the story of a young farmer, Jacobus Van Zyl, who in 1780 lowered himself down an interesting-looking hole he'd found on his land. At this point in the story, a dim red lantern comes on, illuminating a small area further along in the dark. The guide continues, describing how Jacobus, despite not being able see much more than a few feet in front of him owing to his feeble lamplight, felt he'd discovered something significant. He returned to the surface and mounted a full-scale dig and exploration. Suddenly, floodlights come on and a chamber as long as a football field is revealed: Van Zyl's Hall, named in honour of its first guest.

Whether this story is entirely true or told for the benefit of gullible tourists, I'm not sure. I am, however, captured by its romanticism; the idea that a farmer, intent on exploration and adventure, would disappear by himself down a hole into the unknown and return a discoverer of mysteries, now visited by thousands, is surely the stuff of legend.

Being there reminded me of Job 28, one of my favourite passages of the Bible. It likens a man's pursuit of godly wisdom to that of a miner, an underground explorer like Jacobus, intent on discovering hidden gems regardless of the cost or loneliness. I love that we too, though we may never find enticing holes in our properties down which to descend, can experience that same thrill of uncovering buried treasures as we choose to devotedly seek out God and his ways.

Retrieved riches from other subterranean voyages can be found in the town of Swakopmund in Namibia, where there is a 'crystal gallery' housing some of the world's finest underground offerings. Even the façade of the building looks like a shard of glass soaring into the sky. Littered along the pathway from the pavement to the door are hunks and lumps of weirdly shaped rocks.

As soon as we walked through the door on our visit there, out of the sandstorm-inducing wind that whipped down the road, we knew we were entering somewhere special. There, in the foyer, stood what is believed to be the largest crystal cluster in the world. At three metres wide by three metres high, and weighing some fourteen tonnes, it took about five years to excavate from a farm elsewhere in the country. Its multi-edged shape is a geometric masterpiece of prisms and pyramids carefully joined and connected to make one awe-inspiring monument to the creative genius of our God.

In fact, it was out of this sense of awe that the Kristall Gallerie was birthed. An enthusiastic collector, Johannes Adolf Kleynhans began to gather together some of the most impressive gemstones and crystals he could find, and in 1998 the Kristall Gallerie opened its doors to the public, its vision to share God's handiwork with others.

Laid out somewhat like an exclusive art gallery, with paintings and photographs on the walls and sculptural displays occupying the floor space, the discreetly placed lighting glints off the glass cases filled with all manner of precious stones. It is an explosion of purple and green and sparkling white, black, blue and deep brown.

We wandered through the mock mine, where raw uncut lumps of rock were slightly chipped open to display secrets hidden within. Again, careful lighting was deployed to accent the various colours of the gems, giving some indication of the delightful surprise the underground adventurer might stumble across.

A mezzanine level boasted a display of gems from around the world, a kaleidoscopic rainbow of tints and tones. Tiger's eyes and jade from China; opals from Australia; topaz, sapphires, rubies and emeralds. Polished agates, their purple and pink depths revealed, vie with brilliant quartz for attention. I think it was these agates that were probably my favourite – their crystalline, bumpy outward edges looking like nothing more than humble rocks, hiding layer upon layer of increasingly dark and mysterious colour, a universe of space and stars encapsulated in stone.

Each cave explored, each jewel retrieved bears testimony that our God is so much more than just a functional creator. With obvious, intense delight he has designed and formed riches of indescribable intricacy that perhaps no one but he will ever see. It is not merely what we can see and attain that he has fashioned; it is the hidden, the undiscovered, the unreachable, that has received equal attention and care.

Even more, this is just the creation, not the creator. The made is always less than the Maker; the glint of every stone and crystal, the sparkle of every face and facet, is nothing in comparison to the beauty and splendour of Almighty God. Little wonder that Ezekiel could only describe the *likeness* of the glory of God[11] – there is no earthly word or expression, idiom or simile, that comes even close to sufficient for God himself.

Will I progress from fascination with the romantic story of a farmer disappearing down a hole, or the metaphor of a miner seeking gold, and apply my intent and effort to searching for the Treasure who is God, my Heavenly Father? Pursuing his wisdom and his ways, drawing closer to him in the intimacy I was created for; these are to be more highly prized than all the breath-taking delights he has hidden underground. 'Oh, the depth of the riches and wisdom and knowledge of God! How unsearchable are his judgments and how inscrutable his ways!'[12]

A Palace Underground

I chose to seek with determination
with single-focused mind
a palace I had heard of,
a palace underground.

My way at first was hidden,
the path to walk unclear
but as I pressed on timidly,
reassurance graced my ear,

'Continue on this way,
turn neither to the left or right;
though unfamiliar steps you take,
fear not to trip or stumble.'

Eventually, and far from sight,
to this deserted place I came
and at once began my slow descent
through strata of terrain.

[11] See Ezekiel 1:28.
[12] Romans 11:33.

Dark and silent, a stillness pressing heavy,
squeezing past the rock-made walls,
further I was drawn until,
emerging in a sliding rush,
I arrived.

Lit, somehow, by lamps ethereal
and prisms flashing rainbows
this crystal-studded grotto
dwarfs the pride of me.

Colonnades of calcium
made from centuries' drip
surround vast quartzite thrones
agate adorned in purple,
magenta, puce and plum.

Bowing down, in humble acquiescence,
this diamanté-ed crown I've proudly worn
discarded now as trinket brash
in sight of these, earth's treasures.

My quest has reached its purposed end
in a palace underground
And yet in awe of this
creation of a Craftsman
my pilgrimage persists
and I am found, a courtier
in your palace everlasting.

Prayer

Father, thank you that you have hidden treasures deep underground for us to seek out and marvel at.

And thank you for the priceless treasure that is Jesus.

Help me to seek him with more diligence and purpose than others mine for gems, determined to pursue him regardless of the cost; help me to set aside time away from my friends and family in order that I can focus on him.

Thank you that the prize of his presence is worth more than many diamonds.

Higher Ways

God's ways are not our ways, his thoughts definitely not ours. We sometimes forget, in our emphasis on friendship with God, that he is exalted far above all else, an Almighty God with no equal. He doesn't have to do things the way we expect him to; rather, we need to find out how he thinks and operates, and change our perspective accordingly. Thankfully God in his mercy has once again given us clues, natural phenomena or principles that give us a peek into his methods and means.

The Wind that Blows

What manner of man is this, that even the wind and the sea obey him?

Mark 4:41

I'VE JUST COME IN FROM SITTING OUTSIDE, DRINKING A CUP of coffee in the warmth of the winter sun. It's a stunning day, one of those special July days that Durban produces with delightful regularity. There is but a whisper of a breeze disturbing the tranquillity of the trees; the insects buzz from flower to flower with indolent laziness; the sea resembles an Alpine lake, smooth and blue.

It is not always like this. Some days, the wind blows so strongly the waves are whipped into a frenzy of crashing, frothing white. The leaves of the palm tree thrash and thump like the sails on a ship. The windows rattle and the doors bang and the dogs get silly.

Wind is a funny thing. We all know it's present, whether with gentle cooling caresses or can't-stand-up strength. And yet we only ever see its effects, we never see wind itself. It has no shape, no colour, no identifying features that invite recognition. It's uncontainable, untrappable, unstoppable – as any attempt at plugging a draught will testify. It can perhaps be directed or channelled, even harnessed by yachtsman or energy consultant, but it can't be controlled or switched off.

One Boxing Day, we got up early with our packed car and caravan and drove the couple of hours inland to Midmar Dam where we were intent on having a family holiday of sunshine and water. We visit here often and know exactly what everywhere looks like; know the campsite and location of all the stands; know where there is shade, where there is sun. Only, this year was different. We arrived to find that the park management had been removing trees over recent weeks; maybe they were diseased, or simply old, and had to be pruned or cut down. Or so we reasoned. As we continued through the campsite to our reserved spot, there were signs that this was no ordinary display of good husbandry.

There was a caravan with the branches of a tree wedged firmly through its roof. There were piles of discarded white metal frames, twisted beyond recognition from their original purpose as gazebos, tents and sunshades. A couple of boats looked worse for wear. And there were vacant plots, even on the water's edge – an unusual sight for so late in the holidays, when space was hard to come by, even when booked.

We went to find out what was going on. It soon became clear that a disaster of sizeable proportions had hit our holiday destination. It transpired that late on Christmas Eve, a huge, unexpected and uncontrollable wind had blown a path of destruction across the dam and on through the campsite. People had been evacuated from their tents and caravans, told to wait in the brick-built bathroom blocks for safety. One couple were persuaded from their tent minutes before a tree branch crashed through their flimsy canvas roof. Trees that had been part of the landscape for years, strong sturdy trunks seeming fixed till the end of time, were knocked over like skittles in an alley. Camping equipment, even caravans, saved up for over months and bought especially for this Christmas holiday, were shredded and destroyed in seconds. One boat, resting on its trailer near the slipway into the water, was lifted by a gust of wind and thrown, like an unwanted children's toy, twenty or so metres back up the campsite. Once the weakening wind allowed, would-be holidaymakers packed up what was left of their belongings and returned home.

We hadn't been there to witness the wind itself, thank goodness, but its effects were everywhere. Everyone we chatted to had their own version of events, their own stories to tell.

Another time, we decided to take a short weekend break away, again with the caravan and surf-skis, and again to Midmar. We had checked the weather forecast and big winds were forecast at some stage late in the day, but we didn't think we would be affected as we would already have reached our destination. As it turned out, we left late and the wind blew early. Halfway between home and holiday we were caught in the storm, caravan rocking wildly as we pulled it along, surf-skis lurching from side to side on their roof-racks. We needed to stop several times to check and secure ropes and harnesses. Large articulated trucks, using the road to transport cargo from Durban to Johannesburg, pulled over and waited, the danger of being blown over far too real to continue. We passed one that had clearly been driving under a tree as a heavy branch had broken off, landing on its cab and trailer. Thankfully, the driver seemed to have climbed out not too badly hurt.

We had come too far to turn back, but still had some distance to battle through. It was fun – in a crazy, scary kind of way – but it wasn't something we would readily do again. Wind like that is too unpredictable, too potentially dangerous to mess with.

Jesus' disciples knew winds like that. The Sea of Galilee on a still calm day is a beautiful body of water in northern Israel, surrounded by gently rolling hills, grassy banks and pebbly beaches. Fishing boats and pleasure cruisers putter easily along. But then, out of nowhere, the gentle breeze becomes a stiff breeze and then a strong wind and then a howling gale, fomenting the water's surface into a heaving, churning mass of waves and spray.

It was on one such day that the disciples hopped into their boat, with Jesus amongst them, and set out to cross to the other side of the lake. So easy was the passage that Jesus fell fast asleep, content to let the others chat over the day or catch a few fish. Only, catastrophe struck. One of those sudden winds began to blow and the waves rose to within inches of swamping the boat. The disciples, previously relaxed and happy, were now hysterically aware that they might be close to a watery end. Amazingly, Jesus continued to sleep, unaware of the fuss or danger. The disciples, in their fear, got annoyed – how could he, their friend and teacher, their guide for whom they'd left everything, just be ignoring what was going on, resting rather than trying to help? They woke Jesus up, wailing at his lack of care for their well-being. Jesus stood up from where he had been lying and told the wind and the waves to be quiet and to calm down; and they did.[13]

Another time, the disciples had gone ahead of Jesus in their boat while he had stayed behind to pray and recover with his Father from the day's ministry. In the middle of the night, gazing across the water, they spied a figure coming towards them. Peter recognised the figure as Jesus, rather than the ghost the other disciples thought it to be, and cheekily requested that he join his master in his stroll across the water. Jesus, I feel sure with a broad grin on his face, beckoned for Peter to come. He eagerly jumped over the side and, for a few minutes at least, did what no other mere mortal has done before or since; he walked on water. But then it started to go wrong. Rather than focusing on Jesus, Peter began to observe the wind around him, described as a 'strong wind'[14]. He possibly became distracted by the noise, the way his hair and beard were blowing around his face, the size the waves looked. Jesus grabbed and saved him, but it must have been a sobering experience.[15]

Clearly Jesus wasn't as affected, as bothered, by windy, stormy days as we so often are. Could it be that knowing his own authority over the elements, the fact that at any moment he could command them to silence, he didn't need to be afraid? Indeed, he was so secure that he was able to sleep while the waves washed over him.

Jonah's disobedience and subsequent attempt to run from God resulted in a similar squall threatening a similar boat with oblivion. This

---

[13] See Matthew 8:23-27.
[14] NLT
[15] See Matthew 14:22-31.

time, Jonah knew he was at fault and requested he be thrown overboard, ultimately into whatever fate awaited him. Immediately he hit the water, the storm subsided and the sailors were safe.

God has dominion, he has authority, over every storm and whirlwind we can encounter, whether they be a coincidence of our spiritual location or a consequence of our spiritual rebellion. Often though it may be said, it is no less true – Jesus really is in this boat with us, just waiting for us to call on him and watch as he performs a miracle of peace. It is surely only when in the middle of a storm that we get a chance to witness for ourselves God's authority over all things. Jesus is demonstrated as the Prince of Peace during the battle of war, not necessarily during a season of respite.

And what about the Holy Spirit in our lives? In Hebrew, where wordplay is common, the word *ruach* is used both for 'wind' and 'spirit'. The similarities between the two are immediately obvious: they are both unseen and yet experienced; they can be either a powerful force or a gentle presence; neither can be controlled or manipulated by man. In the creation account of Genesis 1, *ruach* is mentioned for the first time: the Spirit of God is seen to be hovering over the waters. Later, in Genesis 6, when God is warning Noah of the impending destruction of the earth, the same word, *ruach*, is used to describe the breath of life found in all creatures. And then, in Genesis 8, it is *ruach* that blows the flood waters away.

The Holy Spirit is *ruach*. He will hover over the chaos our lives can sometimes descend into; he watches over the chaos of the nations as they seem to be in turmoil. He is the gentle breath of God himself, giving life to dry bones[16] and desiccated dreams alike. And he is the mighty wind that blows away the waters of destruction, allowing for new starts and fresh beginnings, rainbows and promises.

So often, I only notice the wind when it's blowing a gale, when my hat is blown off, or when leaves and branches are being hurled from the trees. Rarely, I think, do I stop to enjoy the sweet-smelling breeze of a summer's day, or delight in the calm engendered on a peaceful, still afternoon. Am I perhaps guilty of the same with *ruach*, with the Holy Spirit? Am I only arrested by his more dramatic manifestations, oblivious to his life-giving breath bestowed on me graciously day after day? Do I fail to be grateful for his presence as he hovers protectively over me,

---

[16] See Ezekiel 37:1-14.

knowing when I come in or go out, finding me whether I settle on the far side of the sea or make my bed in the depths of despair?

Ruach

Disturb beyond the surface of my lake-still heart.
Rampage through the murk of my stagnant depths.
Rush over me with a squall and a tempest,
        with a wind that buffets and blows so I can no longer stand
            with the rigidity of upright pride.

Revive in me the love of the fierce and the wild,
        where the pounding pulsating white-water torrent
            is the freedom of chaos caught by my ears.
    and the knowledge, that rising and dipping,
        you hover serenely above.

Breathe into me the breath of your presence
        cooling with grace the heat of the storm
        calming with softness the dead leaf-like rustle;
    and whisper the words that render to quiet
        the wail and the moan, the howl of their protest.
Trusting, I will rest when the waves try to swamp me.
Daring, I will adventure when the wind calls my name.

Prayer

Jesus, thank you that have power to command every wind that blows in my life.

Thank you that you will still the storms when they threaten to swamp me and send refreshing blasts of air when I need to be awakened and stirred.

Help me not only to notice the mighty gusts, but also to pay attention to the breath of your Spirit, as he blows the gentle breeze of your love over me.

Fire, Fire

To appoint unto them that mourn in Zion, to give unto them beauty for ashes, the oil of joy for mourning, the garment of praise for the spirit of heaviness.

Isaiah 61:3

FIRE IS A DESTRUCTIVE BEAST. EVEN NOW, AS I WRITE, I HAVE people in my home clearing up after a small house fire we had a couple of weeks ago. A chair was the only thing that actually burnt, and a window the only item that broke with the heat. But the damage goes way beyond that. The smoke that accompanied the flames was not the nostalgic smell of woodsmoke on a winter's evening. It was a black mass of oily-smelling clouds, billowing and burrowing its way into everything, leaving behind the stain of its presence on walls, fabrics, windows and furnishings. Two weeks and a great deal of water and fresh air later, its reek still offends the nostrils upon entering the room.

In the province where we live, fire is a common occurrence. Much of the coast is planted with sugar cane, from the sweet stalks of which green spikey leaves sprout. As the cane is cut by hand, and as the proliferation of leaves hinders this task somewhat, a controlled burn is undertaken on each field before it is harvested. Throughout the winter months, high plumes of dark smoke indicate, to the initiated, a nearby cane fire. The hills light up, especially at night, with the bright orange glow of flames dancing free and far. Watching the fire on its progress through the field is mesmerizingly hypnotic – sparks catch and rise on the wind, like myriad miniature fireworks displays; the flames rush hungrily from one sweet section to the next; cane stalks, now stripped bare of their leafy coverings, stand silhouetted in row after row of black stripes; and the roar and crackle of this seemingly living monster are heard from metres away.

Cane fires are planned burns, only lit when the wind is in the appropriate direction and with water tankers and beaters on hand to ensure it doesn't spread wildly out of control. But then there are natural fires, those that seem to light up spontaneously along roadways or on hillsides, turning to crispy blackened stubble all vegetation in its path. They wander wherever the wind takes them, burning for sometimes hours, sometimes days. Domestic and game animals alike flee from their reach, and home-owners do battle against their onslaught.

Many years ago, as a child, I was staying with family in Norfolk, England. On driving home one evening, we stumbled across a haystack on fire. We grew more and more excited the closer to it we drove, especially when we realised a fire engine was already on the scene. The fire blazed in full force, lighting up the sky and threatening the nearby tree branches with its anger. Even at the safe distance from where we watched, we could feel the heat, smell the smoke. It was a memorable sight, seared into my young mind by its glowing power.

When the Israelites wandered through the wilderness on their journey to the Promised Land, we read that God presented himself to them as a pillar of fire at night.[17] At Pentecost, the Holy Spirit appeared as tongues of fire above the heads of the apostles.[18] Could it be that God wishes to show us that he is as uncontainable, as unexpected and yet as irresistibly attractive as the flames he chooses to be represented by? Is God revealing that whilst we are captivated by his beauty and warmth, there is danger and holiness too; declaring, as to Moses, that though the burning bush may draw him, yet he should remove his shoes for he is standing on holy ground?[19]

In the first year of marriage, shortly after starting our new life together in South Africa, my husband and I took a long weekend break to explore an area of forest he'd heard of but never visited. We packed our little tent into the car and headed inland to the wilderness camp in the Ngome forest which would be our home for the next couple of days. On arrival, we drove through a forestry workers' village from where we were given access to a track that meandered through beautiful indigenous woodland until terminating at a small clearing which was the camp. There was no electricity; a small wood-burning stove, or donkey boiler, heated the water for showers. Torches sufficed for light in the evening.

We set up our tent and went to explore, walking along root-crossed paths that led, like secret passages, under the trees. We came across rock piles and small caves, waterfalls and streams, all the while surrounded by a tangle of branches and winter-dry leaves. The air was cool and dry, a pleasant change from the humidity of summer, the gentle winter sun flicking and flashing around us as we wandered. Insects buzzed noisily, falling silent only as we approached, as though to pretend they had never been there.

It was only when we reached a viewpoint overlooking the valley below that we saw the familiar black slash of a recent bush fire. Its scar stretched for kilometres, decimating the lush green of the surrounding landscape.

---

[17] See Exodus 13:21-22.
[18] See Acts 2:3.
[19] See Exodus 3:2-6.

We returned to camp a little saddened by our discovery, feeling it somehow diminished the beauty of everything else we had seen and enjoyed.

The next day, we decided to explore a little further afield, and so climbed in the car and went back along the track to the gate at the workers' village. It was here that we met a park ranger, whom we got chatting to about the region and our visit. We mentioned that we had seen the fire damage and how we thought it a great pity that the area had been destroyed in that way. He responded by contradicting our assessment. In fact, he said, the fire was a natural process of rejuvenation that had been occurring almost annually for hundreds of years; the only problem was that human habitation meant the fires could no longer spread as wildly and freely as they would previously have been able to. He said there are records of fires burning across the landscape all the way from the Drakensberg right to the coast, some two hundred kilometres; this would not now be possible, due to the cultivated farmland found in between.

He went on to explain that the fires would burn up all the excess vegetation that sat on the surface of the soil, much of it no longer growing and with little nutritional value for foraging animals. The burn would create a newly-cleared patch of ground from which young shoots could easily sprout and grow. Furthermore, the ash left behind acted as a kind of fertiliser, rich as it is in salts and other vital nutrients. The subsequent growth was stronger and more fertile than that which had previously overrun the area. He urged us to look closely next time we were in an area of recent burn and see how the emerging plant-life now looked.

Some years later, we were visiting Hluhluwe/iMfolozi game park, again in the northern part of KwaZulu-Natal, and again in mid-winter. There had been some extensive fires in the park over recent weeks, and there were great swathes of blackened hillsides visible everywhere. Leaves on trees were brown and curled, no longer pleasant sustenance for any grazer seeking a meal. We began to feel a little sorry for the park's wild inhabitants, when we were reminded of our conversation with the park ranger of long ago. We began to drive towards, rather than away from, the burn zones. To our surprise, there were several buck and zebra browsing amongst the crunchy stalks of fire-devoured grass. On looking closer, we could see what they were nibbling away at; bright green shoots protruded through the baked ground. And not just one or two here and there; a proliferation of new life was gleamingly visible, seeming almost like a scattering of green snow. Yes, the trunks and branches of the small trees and bushes were charred and blackened, but they were no longer choked with the weeds that had become a serious problem in the park over recent years. There was much cause for celebration and future hope in those seemingly devastated hillsides.

In Isaiah 61, the promise of God is that he will replace the ashes of mourning with a garment of praise.[20] The remnants of some of our hopes and dreams, or our relationships that have been destroyed, or our finances that have been decimated, really can appear like nothing more than a pile of ash and soot, bearing witness to the fire that has ravaged through our life. We can feel that future life and fruitfulness is utterly impossible, that our efforts have all been wasted and futile. And yet, for centuries, God has used fire as a means of replenishment, of renewal and restoration in the natural world, so why wouldn't he in the spiritual? The lightning of circumstance may have kindled a desperate blaze, but it has burned its refining power through all within me that restricts my growth with Jesus, leaving behind a deposit that fertilizes and nourishes me far greater than I could have known otherwise. When fires burn, let us look to the Lord for his resurrection.

Phoenix

I hear tell of a sun-bird burning
called, at last, on her final flight home.
From fire she arose and to fire she succumbs
feathers of flame her plumage.

Stillness of death, with only smoke rising,
twisting as wreaths on her grave.

Yet out of the embers a legend ignites
and rises on wings burnished orange and ochre,
soaring above the pyre as it smoulders;
a phoenix reborn from the ashes.

Elsewhere…

[20] See Isaiah 61:3.

smoke billows round in a soot-acrid insult,
choking my breathing and cloaking my seeing;
a blaze catching grasses and branches and leaves
and tossing them free, into the fire of a furnace
where fireworks are moulded and forged;
the roar and the writhe of a manic inferno
inexorable stomp of a monster.

Tomorrow…
the pall of destruction;
the end of life now lost but for memory;
the carcass of dreams lying tortured;
pain hovering loud in the chaos.

But then…
space has been cleared and vision created,
fertility forsaking the barren,
the tender and new –
irrepressible, unstoppable –
tenacious assertion the delight of sweet promise;
the phoenix of hope
reborn from the ashes.

Prayer

Jesus, thank you that you replace the ashes of my hopes and dreams with the beauty of your resurrection life, restoring all that has been destroyed to even greater than it was before.

Help me to trust you, as all around still seems blackened and scarred, knowing that you will do more than I could ever expect or imagine.

Thank you for the shoots of new life I can already see in some places.

Coffee Time

Rest in the Lord, and wait patiently for him.

Psalm 37:7

COFFEE. WE GRAB A MUG OF IT ON THE GO TO GET US STARTed for the day; we chat over frothy cups with friends during the morning and relax with it in the evening after dinner. But how often do we think about how our favourite beverage started out in life?

A few hours' drive south of us is a family-run coffee farm called Beaver Creek. We've visited there often for coffee and cake, either when passing through to other destinations or when we've been staying in the area. In addition to the small restaurant and shop, tours of the farm and roastery are offered to interested visitors. We'd never been on one, so when camping down the road, we decided to investigate.

We met at the restaurant with others of the tour party, keen to get going. One of the farm owners joined us and led us along the path a short distance towards the small trees that were growing nearby. There was row upon row of neatly tended, dark green-leaved bushes; one field of younger saplings being watered by the farm's irrigation system, another with clearly more mature trees, some of which still had a few coffee berries, or cherries, hanging from their branches. Thus surrounded, literally, by the fruit of his life, our guide began to describe his personal journey with coffee.

The family started out with four seeds of the cultivar SL 28 – a plant originally grown in Kenya and Tanzania but adapted to the more subtropical climate of South Africa – and a dream. But dreams alone don't make coffee. After carefully nurturing their seeds into seedlings, and equally carefully planting them in conditions of perfect temperature and ideal soil type, there ensued a long wait of three or four years before the eventual appearance of any 'cherries' suitable for harvesting and processing.

Ripe coffee berries are just the beginning. The fruit is hand-picked and prepared through fermentation and washing, before being placed on sun-drying racks for another two or three weeks. After a further six months of storage, the outer shells are removed and the beans roasted into the form we are familiar with. A quick grind, some near-boiling water, and the coffee is ready.

Beaver Creek is now a thriving farm and business, with seven out of the total fourteen hectares of coffee trees descendants of those original four seeds. But it took the family almost five years before they could even sip their first taste of home-grown coffee. I was struck by their immense patience and perseverance, their determination to reach a goal regardless of the time or the obstacles that were in the way. Farming is not a venture for the impatient or the risk-averse.

The Beaver Creek family had everything they needed to start a thriving coffee farm; seeds, climate and good soil. But they needed one extra ingredient: time.

Many of us have read Jesus' Parable of the Sower a thousand times, seeking to apply its truth to our own lives, ensuring our hearts are of good, fertile soil ready to receive the seed of the word. We work hard at creating and maintaining a healthy climate of godly friendships and mentors in which the seedlings can thrive and grow.

And so, plans and prophetic whispers are planted in our hearts, and we wait with eager anticipation for their fulfilment. Days, months, even years pass, and nothing seems to be happening. We begin to despair of ever making progress, of ever reaping the harvest we feel sure is awaiting us. Abandoning those first seeds to their untended fate, we look for other, perhaps quicker 'crops', losing focus and resolution in the process, finding ourselves becoming increasingly disillusioned and disappointed.

Perhaps instead we need to take a break, sip a cup of coffee and remember that time is also needed. Peter declares that 'God is not slow in keeping his promises, as some understand slowness to be'[21]. I need to trust that God is a great farmer, able not only to plant the seed but also to water it, to nourish it and ultimately to persuade it to germinate and flourish. The Beaver Creek family spent five years not really knowing if their seeds could result in even one cup of half-decent coffee, years that would have included moments of doubt, fear, hope and frustration. Imagine their delight at now looking out across the hillside and seeing a coffee plantation, and a restaurant full of happy coffee-drinkers and a shop stocked with their own products. Their joy is made even more complete after the years of determined waiting. How much more will ours be, when we see before us the reality of what God has previously promised.

There are occasions, however, when seeds seem to grow and prosper with little effort or intervention. Weeds in the garden, for example, are never deliberately sown, or the ground carefully prepared for their benefit, and yet they seem to thrive remarkably when left to their own devices!

---

[21] 2 Peter 3:9.

A few months after our visit to Beaver Creek, we were travelling back from a holiday in Cape Town and stopped for a couple of nights at a campsite in Coffee Bay, in the Eastern Cape. We were towing our large caravan behind our equally large four-by-four, and had anticipated a large-spaced camping site for our occupation. It turned out to be anything but. We turned off the main road, down a short section of steep, sandy driveway, hoping the end of the van wouldn't get stuck as we jerked our way along. We squeezed our way through the gates and entered a fairy dell of tree-covered paths and passages, interspersed along the way with small clearings of flattened ground – clearings more suited to pop-up two-man tents rather than four-berth caravans. We drove on a little nervously, wondering how this was going to work out. Eventually, after getting stuck and needing to unhitch the van and manoeuvre it by hand some of the way, we found a clearing more or less large enough for our purposes.

We set up our temporary home as best we could given the lack of available space, and then began to take a keener interest in our surroundings. We had parked under the shade of a large, spreading tree, one with firm, dark green leaves nestled amongst which were several berries, ranging in colour from pale green to deep red. We didn't think much about the tree at first, but then it dawned on us that we were looking at a wildly unkempt version of the shrubs we had seen all those months before at Beaver Creek – a coffee tree.

What, we wondered, was a coffee tree doing here, metres from the sandy beach and harsh ocean climate? Perhaps, we thought, the name of our location held a clue, so we looked up how Coffee Bay got its name. It transpired that a ship had been wrecked just off the coast in 1893, losing in the process its cargo of coffee beans. These beans washed ashore and onto the beach, where they eventually germinated and grew. No farmer was involved, no entrepreneur planned a new venture, and yet trees capable of bearing fruit just as good as those doted on a few kilometres further up the coast were equally well established.

Sometimes, the seed of God's word is like that – it grows out of nowhere, flourishing in the most unlikely of places. The shipwrecks of our lives or circumstances can be exactly what are needed to radically change the landscape. Coffee is not indigenous to that area of South African coast, and yet a disastrous accident has led to its introduction into one hidden cove of rocks and sand. 'Unless a grain of wheat falls into the ground and dies, it won't produce a harvest.'[22] So said Jesus to his disciples. Can I have faith enough to trust that when catastrophe comes my way and all seems devastated, in fact, seeds are being planted in locations I could only have imagined? Seeds which will develop into a fruitful harvest that otherwise would never have been reaped.

Our Father in Heaven, our God-Creator, is watching over his word to ensure it accomplishes that for which it was purposed, whether it was planted with infinite care or thrown upon the waters and left to float to unknown destinations. Let us be still and wait, knowing that he alone is God.

The Farmer's Reward

In his brown farmer's palm rests the seed of his hopes
        wizened and gnarled and lifeless.
Inert, uninspiring and wholly unsurprising.

Or so it could seem.
For instead he is grasping a miniature world,
        a galaxy of dreams on the verge of explosion;
    a promise of more
        a glimpse of a plan
            and the hint of a multiplied purpose.

But nestled right there in his grip of safe-keeping,
        the treasure he seeks is constrained from discovery,
            trapped in its husk and his fear of its failure,
                dormant and worthless and dying.

Stirring his courage, he lays his prize down
        into its grave of coolness and shadow,
    where, far from his eye of curious impatience,
        a miraculous transforming occurs.

[22] John 12:24.

Till out of the earth, in its own time of choosing
the bursting reward for his waiting and watching
emerges, exuberant and free;
abundant profusion spread out before him
a harvest of plenty from that one single seed.

Prayer

Jesus, thank you for always being so patient with me, even in the times when I wander and get distracted from you and your ways.

Help me to be patient with the work you are doing in my life, trusting that there is a season and a time for everything.

During my waiting, help me to be diligent in the work of preparation.

Thank you that during this time I will come to know you better and understand you more.

Sacrifice and Salt

You are the salt of the earth.

Matthew 5:13

A FEW YEARS AGO, MY HUSBAND CRAIG AND I TOOK A TRIP to Israel to visit my parents who were doing some volunteer work there at the time.

We had a great time travelling around and visiting many places I hadn't been to on previous visits to the area. As I have already mentioned,[23] our day spent with work associates was humbling; to be given an insight into the philosophy and practices of a kibbutz was an incredible privilege. In addition to the rest of the village, we were shown the tower, pockmarked with bullet holes, where the men of the kibbutz had earnestly defended their territory during the 1967 war, taking it in turns to be on the frontline of the battle, and nearby there were ancient Roman ruins, partially excavated.

Back on the more touristy trail, we visited Masada near En Gedi. This, a natural fortress of rock towering above the surrounding valley, was chosen by Herod in 40 B.C. as a safe retreat from possible attack by Cleopatra and her Egyptian army. By 4 B.C. the palace had become a Roman garrison and would remain so until A.D. 66 when it was captured by zealous Jews fighting against their conquerors and oppressors. It became a beacon of safety and refuge for many who managed to escape Titus and his capture of Jerusalem in A.D. 70.

This it would remain until A.D. 72. The Romans, led by Flavius Silva, eventually succeeded in storming the besieged fort, only to be met with the horror of ultimate defiance: 960 dead men, women and children. Under the leadership and influence of Eleazer, every member of the community, bar two women and five children, had burnt their possessions and embraced each other for the last time. Ten men, chosen by the casting of lots, went amongst the people and committed them by sword or dagger to God, rather than have them be captured by the barbaric Romans. Once more, lots were drawn, with one man being left to kill the other nine before turning the sword on himself, thus risking eternal damnation. Self-sacrifice of a level I can barely comprehend.

Not four kilometres away, and visible from the fortress of Masada, lies the Dead Sea. This was our next stop so we made our way to one of the many car parks and 'bathing' spots along its shores. I can't say the Dead Sea is a beautiful place to visit. It's hot and dry with no gently swaying palm trees to provide respite from the sun, or soft, squeaky sand on which to rest and relax! It's rocky and it's salty and it's lifeless. But it

---

[23] See page 26.

is thoroughly unique and surprisingly surreal. We made our way across the shore to the water's edge, treading carefully along the sharp rocks. From the distance, the water looked a dusty, tranquil blue colour, much like any other lake or dam we'd visited over the years. On closer inspection, however, it seemed a dull, lifeless brown colour. There wasn't any waving seaweed, no scuttling crabs, no shyly hiding fish. Instead, every surface was glisteningly encrusted with jewel-like formations of gleaming salt. The sun and waves washed over them, creating a myriad of colour and swirl of patterns.

We picked our way into the water. Every little sore or scratch on my arms and legs immediately started to cry out in protest, causing me to wince more than any antiseptic liquid ever had. A young girl near us began to cry out in real pain as she'd unwisely tried to put her head under the water, allowing the stinging salinity access to her eyes. Her family rushed her out and up to the nearby taps where urgent irrigation took place.

Swimming was out of the question. It was a bit like entering a lake of gloop. There was a tangible thickness to the water which was very unusual. We gave up trying to look elegant and flopped backwards as we'd seen on so many tourist posters and pictures. And yes, you float. Yes, you could read a newspaper quite happily. Though you'd have to try to relax first which might not be quite so easy.

The proximity of Masada to the Dead Sea has recently struck me in a couple of ways. Not only are they opposite extremes – one of the highest points in the area situated so close to the lowest land elevation on Earth – but they highlight a biblical truth that I'd never even noticed before, much less applied to my own life.

In his book *The Covenant of Salt*, H. Clay Trumbull explains that throughout the Middle East, salt had become a symbol of covenant and was used whenever two parties wished to make a binding agreement with each other. The two would become inextricably tied to the other, honour-bound to protect and serve each other until death alone would part them. Thieves and liars, whilst happy to commit other acts of disapprobation, would never renege on a salt covenant.

Whilst we may be somewhat familiar with a blood covenant, such as when two people mingle their blood together by grasping and shaking the cut palms of each other's hand, few may have realised that salt was viewed in the same way as blood. Just as the life of an animal or person is said to be in the blood, salt represented this same life (perhaps because blood is salty to the taste). A covenant of salt, therefore, was as serious and as binding as a covenant of blood. As one partaker put it, 'Your head is now on my shoulders.'

A second essential component of any covenant, whether blood or salt, was sacrifice. Whether it be an animal slaughtered or a loaf of bread broken, the shared meal was part of the deal! Arabs wishing to avoid accidentally making a salt covenant with guests whilst eating would avoid placing salt on the dining table. In the Old Testament, salt was offered along with both the flesh of animals and wafers of grain – giving God, not in fact a dead sacrifice, but one symbolically alive.[24]

Aaron was declared a priest in perpetuity through a salt covenant which God himself made with him;[25] similarly, David's eternal kingship was confirmed by a salt covenant.[26]

Given the cultural and religious understanding of those listening to Jesus at the time, his command that they be 'salt of the earth'[27] would quite possibly have been interpreted in a dramatically different way to our own today. We often think we are to be the added flavour, the piquancy, to an already alive world, or the preservative of something that is essentially sound. But no! The context would indicate that rather, we are to be life-givers to that which is dead (as the salt 'gives life' to the dead flesh of sacrifice). We are to represent an eternally binding covenant of life between God and man through the sacrifice of Jesus.

Perhaps even more profound, this perspective would suggest that we are to live in deep and abiding covenant with other Christians, other 'salts of the earth', committed to each other regardless of difference of opinion or offence taken. And when Paul tells us our conversation should be seasoned with salt,[28] perhaps he means filled with life, promise, truth, love and commitment.

Conversely, when Moses issues warnings to the unfaithful, it is said that the Lord will make their land 'sick with salt'[29]; little can grow and thrive where salt is plentiful. I remember as a child laying salt around the young leaves of some lettuces we were growing in the garden. Why? Not

[24] See Leviticus 2:13.
[25] See Numbers 18:19.
[26] See 2 Chronicles 13:5.
[27] Matthew 5:13.
[28] See Colossians 4:6.
[29] Deuteronomy 29:23.

to flavour the lettuce even before it reached the plate, but to dry up and so kill any slugs or snails that might fancy a sneaky snack! Are we perhaps, as 'salt to the earth', not only life-givers, but also agents deployed to dry up and prevent the thieving works of the devil in whatever situations we find ourselves?

Jesus tells us not to lose our saltiness.[30] How could that happen? Looking at the chemical make-up of salt, we know it is essentially two separate elements fused together. Not to take the analogy too far, but is there a clue here as to what makes us salty or otherwise? When we choose to abide in Jesus – to say, 'Not my will but Yours'; to fully honour the covenant between him, ourselves and fellow Christians – we become blended with him, we become salty. The closer we are to him, the saltier we are; conversely, when I choose to go my own way, to not spend quiet moments listening and talking to Jesus, I move further away from him and therefore become less salt-like. I offer little in the way of life or hope to the world around me.

Thinking again about Masada and the Dead Sea, a height of ultimate sacrifice overlooked the saltiest depth on earth. A coincidence maybe but a poignant illustration that our own saltiness is watched over and overshadowed by the greatest sacrifice of all: the Son of God himself, Jesus.

---

[30] See Luke 14:34.

Salt of the Earth

You are the salt of the earth;
you are the buoyancy on which
the hope of a nation
and a neighbour
floats;
you are the beautifier
the softener
the healer,
the life-blood, the promise, the transfusion;
you are the anaesthetic and the antiseptic
needed on every gaping wound.

You are the salt of the earth;
you are the nutrient,
the encourager of fertility to germinating
sprouting
fruit-filled seeds;
you are the barrier and protector,
the desiccant of the devourer
seeking infant souls
young shoots
old dreams
ancient wisdoms.

You are the salt of the earth
and yet, we ask,
what is this salt?
You and me, the Bread of Life,
combined
entwined
connected.
And not one grain in peaceful isolation
but fused with those around
whose names, like yours, are also called,
whose lives, like yours, are rescued and redeemed
by me.

You are the salt of the earth;
so will you take the challenge
the risk
the ride?
Not to simply do this salting
but to comprehend the need
to hide in me
be made in me
to wait for me
to die with me
to be, with me,
the salt
of this desperate earth.

PRAYER

Jesus, thank you that you call me the salt of the earth, that you have chosen me to represent you and your life to this dying world.

Help me to remember I can't do anything unless I continually abide in you, receiving my saltiness directly from you.

Please help me to be an example of your covenant love to my fellow 'salt-grains' in the church, committed to them even if I receive offense or hurt, learning to walk in forgiveness and love as you do with me.

Determined Wrestlings

There are times in our Christian life that are wonderfully easy and fruitful, when Jesus seems to speak through a megaphone and the Holy Spirit is our constant companion. And then there are times when it all seems impossible; nothing works, we can't hear God, we can't sense his presence, there is no joy or hope and it's all just plain hard. The delightful rain from Heaven has ceased to fall. We can become incredibly discouraged during these times, especially when they are so persistent and seem permanent. Others around us are all well-watered, refreshed, always ready to reap a great harvest, whereas we are dry, lacklustre, depressed and despairing. Thankfully, God is not silent about even these occasions. He declares there is a season for everything, including life and death; he promises he won't allow us to endure more than we can bear or cope with, and he declares that he will remain constantly by our side throughout, even when we don't feel him. Nor are we alone in the experience. Others, with more faith and more fame, have found themselves here. The Israelites, after seeing the defeat of Pharaoh and his army, meandered around the desert for forty years, and John the Baptist spent his formative years roaming the desert regions of Judea. Even Jesus, the Son of God himself, was led by the Spirit into the desert where he was stretched and tested. It seems it's part of a process that we all, if we want to mature and grow into the fullness of what God has in store for us, must pass through. Observations from the created world provide glimpses into the ways of God, helping us face this rite of passage with faith rather than fear. It may take a wrestle with the Lord, we may be left with a limp to remind us of the encounter, but we will be drawn closer to him at the end of it all.

Drought

"When heaven is shut up and there is no rain because they have sinned against you, if they pray toward this place and acknowledge your name and turn from their sin ... then hear in heaven and forgive the sin of your servants, and grant rain upon your land."

2 Chronicles 6:26-27

IN 2017, SOUTH AFRICA EXPERIENCED ONE OF THE WORST droughts in decades. The dams were running dry. The taps were running dry. And in some areas, there seemed little sign of the drought ending any time soon.

It was during the first winter, when the drought was reaching crisis proportions, that we took a family trip from Durban on the east coast right across the country to Namibia in the west. Always a dry time of year for the tropical and highveld zones, it was striking just how dry it actually was. Our first little stop was Midmar Dam, our favourite water-sport and camping spot about an hour away from home. This was woefully low, with the old car park, flooded long ago when the wall had been raised to make a larger reservoir, standing clear of the water line. Small trees and grasses had even begun to reassert themselves – indication that life does go on, regardless. Barbecue stands, low walls, once-tarred roadways all exposed like ghosts emerging from their graves.

We continued; past the next, normally huge dam, used for supplying water to Johannesburg and surrounds. Again, not empty but dangerously close.

On into the Free State, prime agricultural land usually hard-worked and productive, now sitting dusty and idle. Mealie/corn plants, serried ranks of paper-dry brown, still standing alert and to attention yet distressingly barren. Each empty field, each dried-out and cracked farm dam shouting witness to the despair of farm-owner and farm-hand alike. A few, finding no other solution to their livelihoods wasting away before them, opted for suicide as the only way out.

And yet, in that place in my heart where I know God whispers, I sensed hope and a plan. In 2 Chronicles, God speaks specifically about a drought situation, where the heavens have been closed and the rain stopped due to the unfaithfulness of his people;[31] he knows there is nothing like a prolonged drought to assure us that, despite our sophistication, our achievements, our technology and our strategies, we are incapable of controlling something as basic as the weather. We can stamp our feet, jump up and down, read weather apps as much as we like, and it won't make a single drop of water fall from the stubborn sky. Sometimes, in his longing for close relationship with us, God may temporarily withhold his provision or blessings, in order that we would seek him more earnestly, for longer than a quick 'shopping list' prayer.

---

[31] See 2 Chronicles 6:26-27; 7:12.

Across South Africa, churches and communities were driven to prayer with desperate pleas for rain. The national secular media featured articles showing men, women and children beseeching God to be merciful and deliver the country from disaster. I have never experienced anything like this mass 'seeking of his face' before, and it was humbling to be involved. Has not the drought served its primary purpose – to provoke God's people to their knees as they turn to him as their sole provider and deliverer? Outsiders can't help but see where our faith is centred in times such as these.

In our spiritual lives, the same holds true. A drought, whether it be manifest in our finances, our work situations, our relationships or even in our experience of God, cannot be broken by ourselves. We must get on our knees and seek Jesus again, to lay down our ambitions, our pride, and put to one side our solutions and ideas. We need to ask again for a first love to be poured out on us, that we might once more know that sitting still at his feet really is the better way.

A physical drought causes all natural processes to slow down, sometimes even to halt altogether, seemingly never to get started again. Crops fail, harvests don't happen, animals don't reproduce as frequently as the farmer expected. Our personal droughts can make us feel like we're running on a treadmill dripping with treacle – we're going nowhere, and we're going there slowly and with effort.

A distinct feeling I had whilst driving through the barren landscapes of drought-stricken South Africa was one of gratitude of the earth to God. The drought gave the land a chance to rest, to be released from the burden of having to be productive and profitable, whatever the cost to its long-term health. It was like a sigh of relief hanging in the air, faint but discernible nevertheless. We can embrace those times when God takes us into a drought season as an opportunity to rest, to gather ourselves, to be free from expectation and the pressure of performance. There's nothing we can do about it anyway, it's so completely out of our hands, that the earlier we accept this, the less frustrating the time will be.

One final thought on my experience of drought: it is hard work! On the one hand, there is rest from the norm, from the constant cycle of ploughing, sowing and reaping, but on the other, mere survival becomes an effort. Around the country, people were buying bottles of water and driving them to distribution points in their towns so what was collected could be transported to those areas most in need. Farmers with excess feed or silage were arranging to share with those whose animals were starving. In our home village, the water was turned off for all but a few hours each morning and evening. We were all saving bath or shower water in buckets and using it to flush our toilets or wash the floors. Cars and windows had to be painstakingly cleaned with a sponge and cloth, or simply left dirty, rather than doused by a hosepipe as would be normal. Planning was needed for even the simplest of tasks, such as hosting friends for tea – was there enough water in the kettle ready for them to arrive?

In addition to hard work, there has been some hard thinking. A friend involved in the hospitality industry described how the Cape Town hotels, where the drought has been at its most severe, have had to question practices that have long been taken for granted. Wearing white aprons, or providing linen tablecloths and napkins, is not an option when there's not enough water to do the associated laundry; they now wear black and cover their tables in a smart paper. Innovators have found ways to add air to the water as it comes from the taps, ensuring hotel guests can wash their hands whilst using a minimum quantity of precious liquid.

Hard work is needed when we experience our own droughts. We may need to spend longer in prayer, or study the Bible more than we have ever done, as we try to hear what God has to say in our situation. We may have to be more intentional in our interactions with others – whom we meet up with, what we talk about. How we spend our time may be challenged and shifted as we try to find a way to sustainably get through the season. Even so, as we develop and change, we hold onto an expectation of the creative influence of the Holy Spirit as he shows us new ways, new paths, new life in this God-enforced dormancy. The drought won't last forever, no matter how long it may feel; let us ensure we learn and gather and experience all God intends for us while we wait for him to relieve us.

When Times are Dry

Parched.
Really need.
Water.

Cracked.
Like paving.
When?
    Rain.
When?

I think this might be dying;
    or am I resting from
        the toil and labour
            of fertile harvest after harvest;
            of needing to provide for you,
                be pushed by you?
Respite from the battle to produce.

A season to be stripped back
    to be allowed to start again
        with nothing non-essential;
    to reconsider what I'm worth
        what I need
        what I don't;
    stop the 'take for granted'
        of that which I can give;
    discover once again
        what nourishes and succours;
    adjust my timings and my speed,
        my headlong rush
            into exhausted
            destruction.

When?
Clouds come.
Wind blows.
    Rain.

Do I really trust
this time is not forever?
Do I really know
he knows me and he cares
and
he can?

Take stock.
Assess.
Confess.
Remind me that it's not all me
but all, and only, you;
your time, your seasons,
your will, your way.

I really need
you.

PRAYER

Father, thank you that will you often use circumstances to remind me how much I need you; thank you for sometimes stopping the rain so I can realise I am thirsty for you.

Forgive me for trying to keep going without you constantly at my side.

Help me, even today, to return to you with my whole heart, mind and soul, knowing that you will break the drought in your own time, and will care for me until then. Thank you that I can be an example to others of your kindness and mercy through this experience.

The Desert

They shall feed along the ways; on all bare heights shall be their pasture; they shall not hunger or thirst, neither scorching wind nor sun shall strike them, for he who has pity on them will lead them, and by springs of water will guide them.

Isaiah 49:9-10

AT WHAT POINT DOES A DROUGHT BECOME A DESERT? FOR how long must rain be withheld, must dryness prevail, must life seem to pause?

The first desert I ever drove through was in Jordan, when driving from Amman to Petra. I have to say, it was singularly disappointing! I really was expecting the sweeping dunes and crescent shadows I'd seen in pictures of, say, the Sahara. This was just dry and rocky, and rather dull.

Several years later, now living in South Africa, I took my first road trip from Durban to Cape Town, a distance of some 1,600 kilometres, much of which was spent crossing the Karoo desert. Again, I confess to being somewhat underwhelmed on seeing the mile upon mile of straight road, scrubby bush, hardy sheep and those most ludicrous of birds, ostriches.

Since then, I have driven that route several times, and have come to love it. There is something enticingly irresistible about those straight roads stretching ahead into unseen worlds of possibility. When we were last travelling through, we played a game with the children to see who could guess the distance to the next distinguishable bend in the road. The record was about seventy kilometres.

And the scrubby bush? What on first sight looks dusty and lifeless in fact has a vibrancy all its own. The strength of character, almost, to push through the dry, stony ground and be determined to survive, and even thrive, where other lesser plants would curl up and give up, is inspiring. One such plant which captured my heart and imagination is a small speckly aloe, called in Afrikaans a *kanniedood;* literal translation, a 'cannot-die'. It grows almost exclusively in areas like the Karoo, huddled with others of its kind in the shade of larger bushes, often in the rockiest locations. These plants can live for several seasons with no rain whatsoever, the only sign of their suffering being the change of leaf colour, from green to a more red-brown colour. On those occasions when it does rain, the plant produces a profusion of pinkish-red flowers, the nectar from which offers abundant nourishment for those birds and small insects that also inhabit this seemingly so inhospitable terrain.

Surely, we can glean much from meditating on this little aloe! Though our personal droughts may have led us, not into rain and abundance, but rather into desert spaces as bleak as the Karoo, even here we can declare with confidence, 'I cannot die.' As Jesus says of the lilies of the field, not even Solomon in all his splendour was dressed as finely as them.[32] If one insignificant aloe, nestled alongside its fellows in the crevices of a rock, is sustained almost on air alone, how much more can we be assured that we will be fed, watered and cared for during our waiting in the wilderness? Far more even than this, during our sojourn here we can become a life-giver and a blessing to others who wander with us. Our leaves, our outward show of well-being, may change colour; our behaviour, our language, our demeanour may all undergo transformation. But whilst we are planted by the Lord in this place, we *kanniedood.*

It is not only plants that have been created to perfectly suit these arid surrounds. Perhaps the funniest sight in the Karoo are the ostriches. They are really quite ugly birds, with their long, bare necks and equally long, bare legs; eyes that seem to swallow their heads; claws on their two-toed feet; and shaggy plumage varying in colour from dull brown to glossy black. These enormous, flightless birds graze in field-like enclosures somewhat like herds of cattle on a dairy farm. But where cattle munch on lush grass for much of the day, the ostrich has a diet of seeds or shrubby bushes. And pebbles! An ostrich has no teeth, and so must swallow several small, hard objects to aid with grinding and digesting their fibrous food intake in the stomach. If there's one thing in plentiful supply in the Karoo, it's pebbles.

When I am stuck in the desert, with no seeming way of escape, let me remember these ostriches; it may feel like swallowing stones at times, but God is more than capable of providing the best means to perfect nourishment, in whatever situation I find myself. I can rest in the knowledge that I will not starve, dehydrate, shrivel up whilst I am in this place of outward desperation and need. When Hagar ran from Sarah's wrath into the desert to die,[33] God didn't answer her plea for him to just end it all; rather, he opened her eyes to see his provision for her. Is it perhaps that our prayers need to change, from 'let me die' to 'let me see'?

I did finally discover my desert dream, in Namibia. Sossusvlei was magnificent – bright blue skies, burnt orange sand dunes sweeping upward in deep crescent shapes culminating in sharp-ridged tops, and in their concave hollows intense shadows hidden from the sun's penetration.

---

[32] See Matthew 6:28-29.

[33] See Genesis 21:14.

To reach those sights, the intrepid explorer must first buy a ticket from the office at the entrance! Once through, there is a drive of about sixty kilometres across the flat, dry surface of the lake's floor – no longer underwater, except during unusually intense rainfalls when water rushes down the Tsauchab river and can reach this dead end of a salt marsh. Driving along the now-tarred road, our trusty Hilux was drawn inexorably toward the distant dunes, heat shimmering at their base like so many lakes of absent water. It seemed to take an age to finally come abreast of Dune 45, with its car park, toilet and, to us at least, less intrepid explorers. We swept onward, determined to reach the final destination of the alarmingly named Deadvlei.

As we drew closer, the sand became finer, dustier and choking. On either side of the 'roadway', stunted shrubs and miniature trees braved their harsh environment. And then, hidden at first from view, we spied oryx. These antelope, believe it or not, thrive in this their desert habitat, a home offering little by way of grazing or shelter from the harshest of elements. And they are not small beasts; perhaps the size of a cow, at shoulder height they can be up to 1.2 metres. Both the male and female have long horns that resemble pointed rapiers sprouting from their heads. And they have the most beautiful faces – contrasts of black and white, shadow and light, a white mask of Zorro resting on a black nose.

Another antelope local to the area is the springbok, beloved symbol of South African rugby, amongst other things. We saw several of them, painted exquisitely in tan, white and dusty red, curved horns forming unjoined heart shapes above their deep brown eyes. They seemed so delicate, especially in comparison to their larger, more robust-seeming oryx cousins; and yet, their seeming frailty belies their tenacity.

It was only when we turned to our spotter's guide to Southern African mammals that we begin to marvel at the creator's ingenuity when designing these animals. They have an ability to endure weeks, if not months, without water, an invaluable asset in these regions; a springbok can even, in extreme circumstances, live a whole lifetime without drinking from any stream or watercourse. They both survive on the moisture found in desert succulents and shrubs, grazing in the early morning or late evening, when the night dew is at its heaviest. During the heat of the day, they rest in whatever shade they manage to locate, often lying in cooler depressions of the hot sand. Even more remarkable, a springbok cow can delay the birth of her young by as much as a month, should there be just too little water around for new life to thrive.

Perhaps God had something like an oryx or springbok in mind when he said, 'See, I am doing a new thing, I am making a way in the wilderness and streams in the wasteland.'[34] The desert may remain a desert, a wasteland, but God has created hidden resource available to those who seek it. These antelope will wander far in their quest for refreshment, even browsing on moonlit nights should they need to. In those times when we are led into the desert, we need to urgently seek the refreshment that God has there laid up for our survival. It may not appear in the form we expect though; the oryx doesn't necessarily find a hitherto unknown water course, but she does find plenteous liquid in other guises. Once again, our prayer needs to be, 'You have promised streams in the wasteland; Lord, let me see them.'

To return to our own desert journey: we eventually reached a large open area where several cars and four-by-fours were parked. Unsure quite where we were or why everyone had stopped, we went on a quest for information. It turned out that this was the place where those nervous to proceed further into the desert proper in their own vehicles could park up and catch a ride. Us? Nervous? Never! We carried on.

Perhaps those with more nerves were right to listen to them. As we continued, the previously clearly-defined track completely disappeared and we were driving across pure and shifting sand. As we caught up with other vehicles, or encountered those coming back the other way, we became enveloped in swirls of red dust. Visibility was virtually zero; we had no idea what we might be driving into. The tyres swerved and bucked their way forward, my husband fighting with the steering wheel to keep us going straight. It was simultaneously exhilarating and terrifying!

Finally, we reached the next large parking area and joined those others brave enough to have run the sandy gauntlet. We climbed out of the car and got ready for the trek on foot to the dried-up salt and clay pan which was the whole point of the excursion.

Let me at this point say, walking through desert sand is nothing like a gentle stroll on the beach. For a start, there is no mild, salty sea breeze to cool the heated brow nor is there a glistening, rolling sea in which to splash the ankles. It is energy-sapping hot; the ground moves underneath each footstep, making progress slow and frustrating; and everywhere seems far away. We trooped out of the car park and joined the steady stream of folk determined to continue regardless of the pain and

[34] Isaiah 43:19 (NIV).

suffering. And really, some were suffering. We walked along the edge of the dune, the ridge towering above us on the left, a second dune a little way off to our right and, eventually, the dried lake bed below us.

Nothing was growing, no birds were singing; no life except our own seemed present. Yet there, in the basin of this ancient lake, blackened, leafless trees still emerged from the ground. They were twisted, gnarled silhouettes of trunk and branches, some standing upright, others slumped to the ground in resignation. We slithered and slid down the dune into this alien world of petrified carbon and blinding white salt deposit, where time has hung suspended for hundreds of years and luxuriant foliage is a fossilised memory.

Like those ancient acacia trees, we can feel like we're hanging around in the desert of our lives forever. The vibrancy of our hope has become nothing more than blackened stumps, our dreams a crystalline, dead deposit on the floor of what had been a deep pool of clarity. All that seems to be left is an unattainable mirage of life, a march across an unstable terrain in which it is all too easy to get lost and disorientated.

And yet, this landscape is so striking, so intense, that people visit from all over the world; innumerable photos are taken and developed and shared; even movies are made here. It may seem a small consolation, but there can be a beauty to our lives while we wait out our time in the desert, a beauty that is attractive and compelling to a world that thrives on outward success and material well-being whilst slowly drying up on the inside. Namibia has turned this desolate, infertile, unprofitable corner of the country into a vital part of its tourism income strategy; we too can turn our crumbling sand into treasure, adorning our own hearts and decorating the lives of those we choose to welcome in.

We can be assured of directed paths and clear routes through this wilderness, not needing to fear loss or abandonment. The Israelites, when journeying to the Promised Land after their escape from Egypt, were accompanied every day by a pillar of cloud, and at night by fire; they were told when to get moving, when to rest, when to turn right, when to turn left.[35] Jesus, the Good Shepherd of our souls, knows exactly how to communicate directly with our innermost beings, in ways that we recognise and can follow.[36] He will guide us through this place, teaching us when and how to rest, when to push on through the pain and

---

[35] See Exodus 13:21.
[36] See John 10:3.

frustration, whispering, 'This is the way, walk in it,' until we arrive, victorious over the devil and his plans, strong in the word of his power.

Barren Wastes, Green Pastures

Why did my feet lead me here
to this expanse of empty
when yours took you to pastures green
with succour for your soul?

For here I stand on the edge of this trial I must cross,
desperate to fathom the how and the when:
the how will I do this;
the when will it end?

This space where I stand seems too large to inhabit,
too hostile to thrive or survive;
a monotony of distance
and a monologue of landmarks
inspire in my heart confusion and dread:
confusion as to the way I should go;
dread lest I falter and fail.

Already the hopes that I dreamed
and have carried and held
seem to flow like dry sand
through the ineffective clasp of my fingers;
seeing them fall from the grip of my grasp,
watching them descending and dying,
now one with the barren surrounds,
left to be lifted by each wind as it blows
shaping and forming, then shifting again.
An insecure foundation on which I should never have built.

Daunted, somewhat cowed
fully humbled
I proceed on this wilderness way
surrounded,

it seems,
by a shimmer of life,
a mirage of promise which beckons
like the will o' the wisp it is,
always to fade into a disillusioned,
vaporous glare
of disappointment, wasted energy;
despair.

And yet, accepting this sojourn as 'this is what it is',
no longer fighting, resisting and running,
enables me instead to embrace
the meander of paths not of my choosing;
a beauty revealed as magic as moonlight
timeless
time paused
time held by a thread to the moment.
So, slowing down,
letting go
I find sustenance provided in unforeseen manner
hidden before by my self-sufficiency,
found now in my weakness –
jaded eyes wakened to the treasures I'd missed.

Here in the wilderness with nothing distracting,
my ears are attuned to the gentlest of whispers.
'I declare over you that your track may be straight,
a highway raised up for the lost or the lonely
to tread with the passion that comes from compassion
that's lavished on you in this place of your lack,
bestowed with abundance not made by yourself
but drawn from the bounty that's mine.

Though bruised, I'll not break you;
though smouldering, not quench you.
Arise, follow me, for I am the way in this desert
the stream in your wasteland,
your pastures green.'

Prayer

Father, thank you that you are with me, even though I may find myself wandering through a desert.

Thank you that you promise to be my shade by day and my shelter at night.

Help me to trust that you will provide for my every need during my time here.

Give me eyes to see your provision and a heart that knows your presence. Thank you that you can make my life a testimony that will attract others to you as I choose to let you have your way.

Get Ready

...there is a sound of the rushing of rain.

1 Kings 18:41

DROUGHTS DON'T LAST FOREVER, AND DESERTS HAVE boundaries. At some point, there is going to come a change of season, an end of deprivation and hardship and a release of bounty and blessing. But as surely as we make adjustments and realignments during the lean years, we need to ensure we are adequately planning and preparing for when the rains do return.

During the drought in Durban, we were in the middle of re-landscaping much of our garden. We needed to repair a broken retaining wall and so took the opportunity this presented to redesign our pool and decking area. We built a glorious big wall and filled it in behind with much rubble and river sand, culminating in a thick layer of beautiful dark brown top soil and freshly grown grass. We also decided to install an extensive automatic watering system, the water for which would come from harvesting rain from our roof and storing it in three large tanks. This stored water would also be pumped and filtered into our house as a replacement to the rather poor quality and low pressured municipal provision. As a final part of the upgrade, we would enlarge our existing pool by just enough to make it a little more enticing.

This was a great project on paper. We worked through the winter, ensuring sunny dry days on which the work could be started and completed with few weather-related interruptions (Durban experiences summer rather than winter rainfall). However, the plan began to unravel; the rainy season arrived but there was no rain. The local government placed severe water restrictions on our area in an attempt to eke out the remaining supply from the nearby dam. There was no way we were going to be allowed to use normal tap water to fill the pool, much less the tanks which were needed by the irrigation system for our newly planted grass.

We made a plan and purchased recycled grey water which could at least be used for the pool, tanks and irrigation system, so preserving the grass, although we didn't particularly want to use this for household consumption. We just had to wait for rain.

During this time, I held many conversations with God whilst simultaneously looking at the various weather apps and forecasts I could find, asking him for his perspective and trying to twist his arm into sending a downpour. I didn't get the downpour but I did gain some perspective.

In 1 Kings 17, Elijah was led by God to pray for a cessation of rain, and a drought of three years ensued in the region. At the end of the prescribed period, Elijah prophesied that rain would again start to fall from the heavens. So he took himself off to pray this into happening. I was reading this account, for perhaps the hundredth time, when I noticed something fascinating. While Elijah prayed, he kept his head between his knees! He didn't once look up to seek out a tell-tale cloud or lift a wetted finger to feel for a hint of wind. Rather, he maintained his position of humility before God, crying out for salvation and answer, and instead asked his servant to check on the status of the weather.

In our preparations for the start of a new season, are we so desperate to look out for signs that we forget to look out for the Giver of those signs? The point of a drought, as described in Chronicles, is that we should turn our faces back to the Lord, in repentance and earnest entreaty; restoration of relationship and intimacy is God's primary goal in this exercise.

Even once Elijah's servant had seen the 'cloud as big as a man's hand', Elijah himself continued to pray, not distracted by the impending deluge but rather pushing on with his petitions and requests. Sometimes I think we are too quick to observe the first signs of rain and start running for shelter, rather than waiting to actually get wet.

As rainless time passed at home, the ground that we had so carefully prepared for its new carpet of living green became more and more dry and compacted. The grass, so bravely persevering in its attempt to conquer and flourish, began to retreat into nearby shade, and we were left with soil as hard as concrete; no self-respecting plant life would even try to break through that surface. Worse, when heavy rain does eventually fall on this hardened, baked down soil, it just bounces off. There is no penetration through to the roots or seeds nestled safely away from the sun's harsh glare. The soil has become as ineffective as the nearby pavement as a medium for growth and development. We got out a big, heavy fork and started loosening and turning the bare patches of earth in preparation for the rain that we knew would have to fall eventually. It was quite satisfying to work the cracks open and reveal the richer soil below.

As we worked, another passage of Scripture came to mind: 'Sow for yourselves righteousness; Reap in mercy; Break up your fallow ground, For it is time to seek the Lord, Till He comes and rains righteousness on you.'[37]

---

[37] Hosea 10:12 (NKJV).

Fallow, unsoftened hearts become as difficult to produce life as do fallow, unsoftened plots of land. I need to take a fork to the hardened soil of my heart if I am to receive the fullness of the revival rains that will come, rather than have them wash straight off, leaving me unchanged and unfree. To do this, I need to make time to meditate on words of promise from the Bible, to remind myself of any prophetic insights I've received over the years, and to seek daily the softening oil of the presence of the Holy Spirit.

Recently, my husband started working alongside a couple of agronomists. They explained in greater detail why hard, unyielding fields need to be ploughed and broken up – not simply so that tender roots can push through the softened earth, but in fact so that oxygen can more easily reach and nourish those same tender roots. Oxygen won't filter through tightly compacted clay, and so the crop will be starved of more than moisture.

A bird which we have a particular soft spot for is the hadeda ibis. When my parents came to visit soon after I had relocated to South Africa, it was one of their first sightings. They are big, clumsy-looking birds with long beaks and a morning call louder than any alarm clock. The children have a joke that they are the only birds scared of heights, as they cry out in alarm every time they fly! Be that as it may, it's their long beaks which concern us here. They use them to dig deep into the soil in their hunt for worms and other tasty grubs, but the side effect of their poking around is numerous holes bored down into the root-bed of the grass or plants where they're browsing. And holes mean access for oxygen to penetrate. Holes mean life to the hadeda who finds food, but holes also mean life to those roots which crave the food of oxygen.

Our hearts were created to need the oxygen of God's presence, of his love. During a drought or desert experience there is often such a sense of lack – lack of respite, lack of refreshment, lack of God himself. But if the eventual rain that has been promised, the relief we so desperately seek, has any chance of reaching us, we still need to get ready, to break up the unploughed areas of our hearts and determine to prepare for the change that is heading our way. We need to allow the 'hadedas' of the Spirit to poke and penetrate, even though it may be painful; the truths in the word that we maybe don't like too much, the action of praising and worshipping even when we're not feeling joyful, the company of godly friends we'd maybe rather hide from. 'Now it springs forth, do you not perceive it?'; are we ready?

Preparation

Waiting to grow
is so slow
Watching for rain
constant pain
There's nothing that I
though my hardest may try
can do
to undo
this drought that I'm in.

So, helpless and hopeless I sit here and seek
for clouds to come gather and peak
to build and to boil
to rumble and roil;
to split open wide, and then to deluge
for the torrent that's needed is huge.

And stamp though I might
and put up a fight,
still, waiting's the game
bored patience the name.

But is there perhaps a tool in my hand
a job I should do
which later I'll rue
if I leave to the back of the queue?
This ground where I stand
so hardened and baked
will nothing absorb, unless raked
with the strength of a hand
which believes
in the rain that will fall.

Rather, I think,
than to think on what's lacking
my focus should be on your word that's unflagging
a promise you spoke in the hardest of times

of hope and of rescue from these punishing climes;
where, restored by a break of the season we're in,
the life that was dormant will once more begin
to flourish and thrive
be fruitful, revive,
reaping a harvest that others will know
is all by your doing, from you came the flow
that hydrated the desert
that watered the dirt
that ended the drought I was in.

PRAYER

Father, thank you that you will send your rain when you are ready.

Help me to faithfully prepare for your breakthrough and not become distracted by looking for the sign of clouds.

Show me areas that I still need to plough and tend in order that I could receive all that you have in store for me.

The Rain

Praise the Lord, all his works everywhere in his dominion. Praise the Lord, my soul.

Psalm 103:22 (NIV)

WHEN IT RAINS, IT POURS! HAVEN'T WE ALL SAID THAT A thousand times, usually when things have gone horribly wrong and we wonder how that happened.

According to one of the water authorities in Durban, there is no statistical evidence that droughts are followed by an intensity of rainfall that leads to flooding. But it does seem to happen quite frequently. Certainly, once it finally started to rain at home, we had more than enough. My son and I went out with buckets and large black bins to collect as much falling rain as we could; we were soon soaked and our vessels overflowing. Our water harvesting tanks were also inundated with run-off – so much so, in fact, that one of them buckled under the weight of the water and collapsed, sending litres of water rushing down the hill. It was chaos, but a kind of glorious, dripping wet, exhilarating chaos after so many months of dryness.

A few months later we went with friends to a private game park. We had been staying nearby, so we drove the few kilometres to our rendezvous, where we stocked up with provisions for our adventure, then continued to the gate of the park. We signed in and made our way to the accommodation. This was to be no bush campsite but rather a luxurious, many-roomed lodge, which was for our exclusive use.

Also for our exclusive use was a ranger and off-road spotting vehicle. Early the next morning, we got up, grabbed a cup of tea and clambered up into our seats. Off we went, to explore and investigate. It was quite cool and somewhat damp, but wrapped in our blankets we were well protected from the elements and excited at what lay in store.

We rumbled slowly along the dirt roads, the green of the trees and shrubs a deep, intense tone after the recent rainfall. We stumbled across a herd of buffalo, performing their morning ablutions in a large, muddy watering hole, delight sounding in every snort as they enjoyed the process. Further along we were treated to the rare sight of five or six lions snoozing on the banks of a dry riverbed. They lay, perfectly relaxed, spread-eagled in the sand, with just a twitch of a tail or flick of an ear indicating life. Contentment reigned.

Continuing our drive, we heard birds calling to one another through the ever-deepening mistiness. The leaves on the trees began to drip, stray branches sprinkling water over us and our open vehicle as we passed.

After a brief coffee stop on the top of a small, treeless hill, we moved further into the game park. Over the radio came the crackle of information that there had been a sighting. Of what, we asked? A female cheetah and her three cubs; rare, in that cheetahs are only infrequently seen; rarer still to have three cubs accompanying her. The ranger explained that in all probability, only one of those cubs would survive to adulthood, the mother having to fend not only for herself but also to keep guard over the little ones, a near impossible task.

We found where the cheetahs were wandering through the damp grassland, honoured to witness her progress to the safety of the trees. The cubs played as they ran along, oblivious to the potential dangers that lay all around; the mother, by contrast, all erect neck and head, alert to the slightest unexpected movement or sound nearby. We turned off the idling engine and simply sat and watched, in awe of the privilege of being there at just that moment.

As we sat, cocooned in our rain jackets and blankets, sounds muffled by the descending clouds, I was overwhelmed to the point of tears. In so many places throughout the Bible, creation is given a voice, a means of expression: the trees of the field clap their hands,[38] the stones will cry out in worship if we will not,[39] creation groans for the revealing of Jesus glorified.[40] At that moment, I heard, audible in my spirit, the worship of creation for the creator. Thanks arose from the trees and the grasses as they drank in the sweetness of falling rain; adoration and joy echoed through the melodies sung by dozens of unseen birds; gratitude for provision was heard in every snort and twitch from every animal. It was an insight that stirred me to the core: *all that is around me is an orchestral masterpiece of perfect praise offered to him who is the Life-giver, the Sustainer, the Source. How can I remain silent?*

When barren blue skies eventually billow with clouds and the first fat drops of rain plop to the dusty ground, there is deep-breath relief. In Africa, it is accompanied by a scent unlike any other – of warm earth being gently cooled, of dust particles bouncing into the air. For a few moments, we pause to see if this is real or just a passing taunt. Then the drops fall quicker, closer together until they are a torrent tumbling from a slashed-open storehouse of waterfalls and rivers and dams.

Our droughts, our deserts, our dry seasons can be replaced with a monsoon from heaven that drowns our despair and hopelessness in a moment. A 'flash flood' is called so for a reason; it flashes, out of

---

[38] See Isaiah 55:12.
[39] See Luke 19:40.
[40] See Romans 8:22.

nowhere, sweeping along everything in its path, clearing the rubbish that has built up in the river courses and gorges through which it rages. Trees, rocks, boulders; nothing withstands its energy or its purpose. We will be forced to our knees in praise, adoration, worship, awe as Jesus overwhelms and overpowers us with his beauty and his presence.

Keep holding on, keep preparing – the rain is coming!

Exaltation

How can I not,
together with fibrous roots
sinewed branches
greening leaves
with gratitude and reverence
praise the name of God the King?

For you are the one who spoke this life:
El Chuwl, Elohim, the author, the creator,
Jehovah-Bore;
birthing out of nothing this all.

You are the timeless, the eternal
the Alpha and Omega
existing before it was
remaining ages after it will be.
Attiyq Youm, Ancient of Days
enthroned, enrobed;
before whom our crowns are flung
our hearts, prostrate
succumbed, submitted.
Pre-eminent – El Elyon
Majestic ascendance – El Shaddai.

Beyond the comprehension of my earthly simplicity
El Deah, you who know
the mysteries of infinity
the secrets held by souls, like mine.

Unto you we lift our sighs
our cries
Oh, Yahweh-Raah,
shepherd of us, your sheep;
in kindness leading me to pasture's sweet
nourishing me, pausing me, restoring me.
cleansing me with crystal fountains
from you, my source, provider,
Jehovah-Jireh.

I am undone by the compassion of this King –
the Lord who sees, El Roi –
and seeing, comes to save;
never forsaken, never abandoned
overshadowed by this Jehovah Shammah.
Omnipresent.
Ever there.

Banner of victorious grace,
Jehovah-Nissi,
to whom our hearts may rally
and turn from dormant slumber.
Alive once more to rainbows of his glory.
The battle won, the war complete.

Awe and adulation
devotion, adoration
glorification
arising in a tapestry of sound from all created masterpieces
to you
our all, in all, through all
Yahweh
I AM.

Prayer

Father, I join with the rest of creation in praising you, for you are wonderful in all your ways.

You are worthy of my constant praise and adoration, and I love you.

Wonders Revealed

After all our meanderings, from the first thundered whispers through to our final determined wrestlings, we come at the last to this, the hem of his garment, the outskirts of his glory. The crowd now absent, our hearts stilled within us, ready, like Elijah, to be called to the entrance of the cave and be permitted deeper intimacy with our God.[41] It is surely here that we are silenced by the wonder of his presence.

[41] See 1 Kings 19:12 (NKJV).

Castles in the Mist

Behold, I stand at the door and knock. If anyone hears my voice and opens the door, I will come in to him and eat with him, and he with me.

Revelation 3:20

I HAVE ALWAYS LOVED CASTLES. WHETHER THEY BE THE Cinderella chateaux of France or the Macbethean ruins of a Great Zimbabwe, it matters not much. I love the mystery infused through them, the sense that others, grander, more powerful, statelier than I have passed through and made them the centres of kingdoms.

I love the towers from where Rapunzel has let down her hair, where spiral stairs cause my head to spin and my legs to wobble, with little slots of windows spaced at regular intervals so I can see how high we rise and how majestic the view. I love the worn stone steps and the pitted rock walls and the wooden doors that always seem to be closed at the top.

I love the kitchens and workrooms, deep in the hidden realm of these great mansions. I imagine the banquets prepared, the rush and the fuss of guests and dinners and feasts. The heat, the tension, the exhaustion and the delight of accomplishment.

The ancient ruins of Great Zimbabwe, now lending their name to an entire nation, are perhaps the most awe-inspiring of any palace I have explored. Our first sight as we drew close was a bumpy road and a stony car park with a guarded hut for entrance fees – one price for locals, another for Southern Africans and still another for the rest of the world. We parked next to a couple who were travelling through the Zimbabwean landscape in an entirely unsuitable hired white sedan car. After their third puncture, they decided they had been sold a con and would never return to the area again.

It was genuinely cold as we made our way along the pathway leading through the waves of wet grass, past the suitably modern toilets, to the start of the ascent to this hilltop fort. Built, it is believed, between the eleventh and fifteenth centuries by the ancestors of the Shona people, the castle mound is skirted by a towering wall capable of withstanding the winds, the rains and the baking African sun, year upon year upon year. Its grey perfection honours the skill and dedication of its makers, whilst the pathways and steps that lead upwards to its summit testify to the footsteps of thousands.

We followed those pathways and steps, ascending ever higher into the cloud and mist. Furls of white damp floated over the rocks and grassy edges, shrouding us in mystery. Roaring fires were needed here, animal skins and woven blankets. Long-silenced songs are held captive in the ever-listening walls.

The fort itself was somehow blanketed and cloaked by the thickness of the mist. It was hard to discern the edge or gain an accurate perspective of how high up we were. It was even difficult to correctly evaluate how intimidating a site this would have been in days gone by, towering as it would have in solidity and permanence far above every mud and straw hut in villages for miles around.

Castles and fortresses are very much the invention of man, not the Father's creation that we have been looking at throughout these pages. However, our own hearts can often be like castles – strongholds locked up against invaders, hidden motives like secret passages and chambers, sometimes so twisted and complex that we ourselves forget how to find the centre. We might hide our hearts' defences behind the mist of appearance, saying the right things in the right way at the right time. But there is one who knows the true nature of our castle-hearts – Jesus, he who stands at the door and knocks, waiting for us to open to him.[42]

As we meditate on God's ways and dealings with us, drawing on the life around us for inspiration and understanding, perhaps we become a little more able to entrust ourselves to him, to take courage and unbolt the door, opening it wide to his presence. He promises to enter with abundant provision, declaring that his desire is to sit and eat with us, to enjoy our company as one friend would another. And his assurance is perfect peace for all those who welcome him,[43] our own-built fortifications no longer necessary for our well-being.

---

[42] See Revelation 3:20.

[43] See Isaiah 26:3.

He Knocks

Damp curls as tangible as woodsmoke
blanketing to silence
softening and blurring the edges
of this fortress of a heart I've established.

Castellation proud and permanent
labyrinthine passages twisting, winding
reaching chambers long forgot
and doors sternly resisting entry.

Into this defensive stronghold
cloaked in mist and fog
his footfalls barely echo
so gentle is his step;
till standing at the firmest shut of any barrier found
he lifts his hand to knock.

Persistent thud of palm on wood
awakes my sleeping soul.
Rushing, fumbling, nervously unlocking
I bid him enter in.

He steps across the care-worn threshold
and carries with him a breeze as fresh as any ocean air
bright, clear, true;
easing memories of darkened nights
blowing dust off long-left dreams
and illuminating every darkened corner of me.

PRAYER

Jesus, thank you that you stand at the door of my heart and knock.

Thank you that you want to come in and eat with me, to have fellowship with me.

Help me to open any doors which are still closed to you, trusting that you are here for my good and not my harm.

Jesus, you are welcome here.

His Voice

...and his voice was like the roar of many waters.

Revelation 1:15

OUR VISIT TO ZIMBABWE WOULD HAVE FELT SOMEWHAT incomplete without a trip to Victoria Falls. The only downside was that we were based in Harare, with family, whereas we needed to be on the other side of the country, a drive of about 800 km. Undeterred, we climbed into our trusty four-by-four and set off, with strict injunctions to stay on the main road ringing in our ears.

We managed to obey for the first hundred kilometres or so. But the roadworks, trucks and other delays were getting us down, and there, just a little way ahead, was the right-turn that would take us on the shorter, quicker, strictly-warned-against alternative route. Of course, we turned right.

Our initial thought was that we'd made a huge mistake. The untarred road stretched before us like so many frozen waves of sand and dirt. No matter what speed we drove, we couldn't avoid being jiggled to our bones; too slow and the bumps became little hillocks to be climbed one by one; too fast and we were a blur of rattling car and shaking bodies. To add to our woes, at the entrance to every small town there was a police roadblock. We had to stop, produce a driving licence and the necessary paperwork required to be a road traveller from 'abroad' whilst proving that all the essential elements of the car were in good working order. Nerve-rackingly, our rear brake light wasn't, so we created an illusion of function by turning on the headlights when the policeman checked at the back, fervently hoping his colleague wasn't going to be simultaneously standing at the front and thus reveal our trick!

It took us the best part of two hours to cover approximately one hundred kilometres. At this rate, we were going to arrive at Victoria Falls after midnight.

Mercifully, we reached a small stretch of tarred road after which the dirt had been graded and was relatively smooth-going. We sped up.

It was perhaps the most memorable of road journeys I've undertaken. We passed huge areas of what had obviously been highly productive examples of agri-business, farms that were now left for the trees and wandering sheep to occupy. There was evidence of well-tended fences, enclosures of orchards, driveways to once flourishing farmsteads, all now abandoned. We speculated where the owners may now be, what decisions they'd had to make when leaving, and how long they'd had to prepare their departure. My husband's own brother-in-law's family had been farmers in another region of the country who had no choice but to abandon all they'd worked for and start again across the border in Zambia.

It was a sobering, heart-disturbing trek.

There were lighter moments of course. At one point, we came across a road sign clearly designed to warn of the dangers of elephants up ahead. Somewhat bemused, we continued carefully, only to find ourselves on the edge of a pretty steep drop into a dried-up river from where the bridge had disappeared. Wondering what to do next, we found a less steep climb down to the riverbed which we were able to negotiate with relative ease, being mindful of the possible elephants lurking unseen in the nearby bushes (it is surprising how well an elephant can lurk unseen!)

On another section of the road we saw strange white, cloudlike puffs hanging on the small branches of the trees we passed. We excitedly tried to identify the crop in question, surprised that cotton could be grown in these parts; only to discover, a little further down the road, a truck carrying fabric bales of cotton, the sides of which had been ripped open by the sharpness of protruding twigs.

We also passed another truck which had been in an accident of some sort – the drivers sitting somewhat stunned beside a newly-lit fire, awaiting rescue. We wondered how long that rescue would take, being grateful that nothing untoward had happened on our own travels in such faraway places.

Finally, we returned once more to tarred road and made our, considerably faster, way to our destination. The sun was setting by the time we arrived at the somewhat disorientating civilisation of the town – there was a small airport, designed for overseas visitors to fly straight into without having to traverse vast distances by car. The road was wide and well-maintained, and directions and signposts were plentiful.

Once we'd found our campsite and offloaded some of our luggage, we went in search of the bridge that crosses the Zambezi from where we would catch our first glimpse of the famed waterfall. We drove through the town to the border post (between Zimbabwe and Zambia) and parked the car. We would continue on foot from there.

We walked past the guards in their offices and headed towards the centre of the hundred-year-old bridge. And what a bridge! It was built in 1904 on the instructions of Cecil Rhodes as part of his ambitious plan to build a railway line from Cape to Cairo. His intention was for the train passengers not just to see the waterfall as they crossed the river but even to feel its spray. The steel components had been designed and fabricated in England then shipped to Mozambique, before being transported along the burgeoning rail network to site. The final day of construction arrived, only for the engineers and others to realise, with immense consternation, that it didn't quite fit together. It was a disaster; one that would have to wait till morning to resolve. Morning came, and miraculously the protruding part had slipped into place, as the metal had contracted just enough over the cool of night to fit snugly where it belonged.

The following day we set off to explore the Falls themselves. Whilst not the highest or the widest waterfalls in the world, Victoria Falls still lays claim to be the largest by virtue of a combination of both. The Zambezi river flows gently and widely across the flat upper planes only to suddenly drop off the edge of what seems a giant bite from the landscape. The water pours forth with a frothing, foaming intensity that soaks all within range, providing the most powerful display of aquamarine energy I've ever seen. Once at the bottom, the river meanders through the gorge around twists and bends before disappearing from view completely.

A year or so later, when I was at home with my Bible, I read the following words in Revelation: 'Then I turned to see the voice that was speaking with me … and his voice was like the roar of many waters.'[44]

This was now more to me than a helpful but unexperienced metaphor. I thought back to what it had felt like at Victoria Falls, how the noise began as a gentle, distant rumble as we approached until it became, when standing soaked and blinded right on the edge, a deafening, rushing, booming roar, our own voices completely overwhelmed into silence.

The voice of Jesus is like the sound of Victoria Falls, only even they are surely too quiet, too tame, to do him justice. His best friend, John, fell to the ground as though dead when he saw and heard that Voice. When we ask our God to speak, are we ready for him to do so, to be so wildly beyond our expectations and experiences that we are literally floored by his strength, by the 'word of his power'[45]?

[44] Revelation 1:12,16.
[45] Hebrews 1:3.

I Turned to See the Voice

Billowed clouds of distant mysteries
like smoke from a thousand village fires
round which elders wrapped in blankets
pipe pinched between sun-cracked lips
watch children skip and hop
and women work the time away
wishing for their turn to sit and watch and warm.

But these clouds are not the silent fluff of floating flames.
These clouds rumble
like the drums of barefoot armies
stomping heat-baked soil of ancestors' hidden pathways;
thunder of the ancients.

Drawn by mesmerising promise
of something stronger
deeper
than all before
I find I cannot remain in this one place
of distant wondering wonder

Hooked, I am reeled in;
transfixed, I am wooed
to a fairy-land of emerald-fingered ferns
glistening with the drip of living diamonds
of gems and jewels
and prismed light –
and noise.

A baritone, a treble
a tenor.
A choir of endless
timeless
concert.
A cathedral of acoustic eternity,
its own self
sufficient audience for performance.

Magnetic compulsion and I am beckoned by the rush and plunge,
the froth and foam,
the abandoned recklessness of over-the-edge meanderings;
exuberant, inexorable
the tumultuous tumble of laugh-out-loud inevitability,
that unstoppable downward drop;
until I stand on ground so holy
that drenched, I am waiting
soaked, I am captured
deafened, I am silenced
as now I am sheltered
in the deluge of a cloud that thunders.
No questions, no tears
no misunderstandings
no fears;
no falsehood, no pretence
no defence.

Blinded, all is overtaken
undone
overcome
by the infinite
ancient
eternal
sound of rushing waters that is
you.

Prayer

Jesus, your voice is as the sound of rushing waters.

Here I silence myself and wait for you to speak, to overwhelm me in the torrent of you.

My Voice

O my dove, in the clefts of the rock,
in the crannies of the cliff,
let me see your face,
let me hear your voice,
for your voice is sweet,
and your face is lovely.

Song of Songs 2:14

MY FIRST SIGHTING OF PETRA WAS WHEN I WAS A TEENAGER, in Jordan on a family visit to a friend who was working in the country at the time. We took a long bus trip from Amman where she lived, through the desert to the Wadi al Rum area. The arrival at the entrance to Petra was buzzing with activity – a flat, dusty area around which coachloads of visitors were corralled in varying stages of excitement or exhaustion. Amongst them wandered men from the nearby village, heads wrapped in chequered squares of red, black and white fabric, noisily leading ponies slung with colourfully woven saddlebags and blankets – all ready to take their burdens of touristy glee to the bottom of the ravine, the start of which was just glimpsed around the corner.

We opted to walk on our own feet rather than on the ponies. It was a gentle descent, although caution was needed, both to avoid the treacheries of loose rocks on dusty ground and being trampled by the careering, shouting horsemen intent on returning to the start to collect more passengers before their mates could beat them to it. Rock walls rose on every side and the heat of the sun no longer penetrated to where we walked. The manic chattering of eager pilgrims became a more subdued murmur of awe and anticipation as the sense that we were travelling towards a destination of near mystic quality deepened.

And then we saw it. Flanked on either side by a gateway of rock formed from the sides of the gorge through which we walked, a dusty pink edifice of Hollywood proportions gleamed with rosy light as the sun caught its façade. Around one last corner, and the path opened into the wide space that appeared like a temple courtyard at the base of the stone steps of this most impressive of entrances. The 'Temple of Doom' of Indiana Jones fame; el Khazneh, the probable temple-tomb of an ancient Nabataean king from the Hellenistic period.

And perhaps it's this very antiquity that adds to the Rose City's mystique and allure. There is a sense of walking in history's footsteps, of following paths that others have worn. At the time of the judges of Israel, Sela, as it was then called, was known to form the border of Amorite territory;[46] later, during the reign of Amaziah, king of Judah, the city was captured by war and taken by the Israelites.[47] Most beautiful of all is the promise spoken by Isaiah the prophet that the people of Kedar, descendants of Ishmael, living in the wilderness and cities that included

[46] See Judges 1:36.
[47] See 2 Kings 14:7.

Sela, will one day turn to the Lord in worship and sing for joy on those very mountaintops.[48] Given that the current inhabitants of the region are still descendants of Ishmael, and Muslim in belief, this is particularly significant.

Petra is not a place of quiet contemplation! There are tourists and tour guides everywhere, each vying for the attention of the other. There are horses, camels and flies. The restaurant at the far end of the ancient city is modern, always busy, and noisy. Village children, barefoot and dusty, follow behind each group of visitors, calling alternately for sweets or sales; bottles filled with stripes of indigenous sand compete with leather(ish) belts or those ubiquitous saddlebags, all hoping to be exotic enough to attract the dollars of eager sightseers and keepsake-purchasers.

When I revisited with my husband many years later, the symphony of sound that is a major tourist destination all got a little overwhelming. We decided instead to follow a path up and away from the main routes and pathways; steep steps, created by the feet of sheep and shepherds alike, led upwards to the desert plain above. Here, finally, there was peace. A few others had taken similar excursions and could be seen wandering around the top of the gorge, seeing the city from a vantage point of distance and calm. A local man came riding past on his stocky brown horse. Small silvery-green succulents sprouted out of the hot sand whilst lizards warmed their internal cold on the sun-whitened rocks. Following a track that led back up the gorge, we looked down on the people below as they ooh-ed and ah-ed their way towards the unexpected climax of their journeys. Up here, the chatter was muted, the air finer, the whole encounter somehow more ethereal, restful. Is this perhaps why Jesus often climbed a distant hill when seeking the solitude of prayer? Or why, on those occasions when God met with individuals such as Moses and Elijah, or Peter and John at the time of the Transfiguration, he did so on mountaintops and rocky crags?

Besides the man-made caves and ornate temples, Petra is also a city of cracks and fissures fashioned by the power of the elements; sun, wind and rain the tools in the Master Carver's hands. Old Testament references to being hidden in the clefts of rocks, to flee like doves to these refuges of cool and safety, suddenly have resonance and meaning when in such a location; we can learn from these regular inhabitants of smaller temples.

---

[48] See Isaiah 42:11.

Doves won't settle where there is noise or conflict; they seek out places that are secure from disturbance. Once such a nest is found, these birds, more than any other, have a remarkable homing ability – witness the pigeons, members of the same family, used during times of war as winged messengers, able to navigate back to HQ with news and instructions.

Doves are not only drawn to return home; they are also drawn to one mate for life. When in Song of Songs the lover likens his beloved to a dove, it is perhaps this single-hearted devotion that he has in mind. Even the eyes of a dove are single in their focus; they have no peripheral vision and so are consumed by that which is in front of them only, free from the distractions of all that lies on the margins.

Jesus, as the Lover of our souls, calls us to be his beloved, to respond as doves to his wooing. May it be that our hearts would know where they truly belong and are safe – hidden in secret places with him who has eyes for us only and on whom we gaze with eternal gratitude.

Come Away

Come away, my love, my dove
from your weary wanderings
in valleys of shifting shadows
where the horsemen's mournful keening
echoes the dirge of once dying hearts,
bespeaks the cries of older souls.
Away from the place where the feet of kings and warriors
have trod and fled and fallen,
where the battle has burned and raged,
spilt the gore of life
into pools of uncaring depth.
Out from where the dust has clung and cloyed,
where despair
has ruled.

Ascend, my love,
to be free of all assaults on screaming
scare-filled
senses;
and seek instead the stony stepways,
these secret places of the stairs.

I incline my ear to this one who calls
he who sees and knows
and choose to walk the unknown way
of shepherds
leading sheep.

Come away, my love, my dove
from the temples and the dwellings,
from the push and shove
the 'Look here', 'No there', 'Hurry on'.
Be refuged in these
my rock-hewn cotes
citadels of kinder air

where clamours for attention
muffle, mute,
become ripples of benign disturbance.
Rest sweetly and hush
the hurrying of your heart
and breath deeper in this,
the coolness of an altar's cave.

But hide not your face from mine
for on you,
my eternal affection,
I long to set my gaze
to watch for any passing shadow
or the sunshine of your smile.
And still not your voice
lest I should miss
that which burdens you
unseats you
disquiets you;
or
delights you
ignites you
I love to hear your laughter.

Uncage my homing heart
unfetter my affections
that I would rise with burnished, Son-drenched flight
to where you wait

PRAYER

Jesus, thank you that you shelter and hide me in the cleft of the rock that is you.

Thank you that you love and cherish me and want to hear my voice.

All I can say is, 'I love you'.

What Shall I Read Next?

Publisher's Recommendations

A Leaf Between My Toes
Jane Upchurch
ISBN 978-1-907509-56-8

Wonder is a discovery that transforms a dull day. It enlarges our hearts so that they fill with the qualities we honour. It is a link with what is sacred; it is a way of worship. If we take time to notice, to listen, to wonder, we are called out of ourselves. It can happen as we drive to work or sit quietly at home. It can happen on holiday or as we walk the dog. It can happen in our garden. Jane Upchurch's insightful poems flow naturally from her heart of wonder as she observes the natural world around her. From her 'garden sanctuary' she recognises how God expresses himself through all that he has made; the gifts we take for granted often hold secrets of remarkable wisdom...

Raised from Dust
Alison Stedman
ISBN 978-1-911086-82-6

In this collection of poems, Alison takes us on a journey around the world, from the familiar sight of a homeless man on the streets to the wonders of Asian countryside and culture. With sentiments echoing Ecclesiastes, she mourns the transient nature of our lives and all that we see around us. She then flips the coin and explores birth and rebirth, leading to a hope that transcends our temporal existence here on earth.

Books available from UK bookshops or
www.onwardsandupwards.org